What you need to know about the National Tests

KEY STAGE 3 NATIONAL TESTS: HOW THEY WORK
Students between the ages of 11 and 14 (Years 7–9) cover Key Stage 3 of the National Curriculum. In May of their final year of Key Stage 3 (Year 9), all students take written National Tests (commonly known as SATs) in the three most important subjects: English, Mathematics and Science. The tests are carried out in school, under the supervision of teachers, but are marked by examiners outside the school.

The tests help to find out what you have learned in the key subjects. They will also help parents and teachers to know whether students are reaching the standards set out in the National Curriculum.

Each student will probably spend in total around seven hours during one week in May sitting the tests. For each subject, you will probably do two test papers. In the English test, one will be a Shakespeare paper.

The school sends the papers away to external examiners for marking. After being marked, the papers are returned to the school and results reported to you and your parents by the end of July. With the results of the tests, you will also receive the results of assessments made by teachers in the classroom, based on the work you have done during the school year. You will also receive a summary of the results for all students at the school, and for students nationally. This will help you to know how you are doing compared with other students of the same age.

The report from your school will explain to you what the results show about your progress, strengths, particular achievements and targets for development. It will also explain how to follow up the results with your teachers and why the test results may be different from the teacher's assessment.

WHY THE KEY STAGE 3 NATIONAL TESTS ARE IMPORTANT
It is very important that students do as well as they can in their National Tests. Good test results, together with a positive report from the school, will ensure you are placed in a higher group for your GCSE courses. In turn, this means you will have the opportunity of achieving the highest grades in your examinations.

LEVELS OF ACHIEVEMENT: KNOWING HOW WELL YOU ARE DOING
The National Curriculum divides each subject into a number of levels, from one to eight. On average, students are expected to advance one level for every two years they are at school. So, looking at the table overleaf, you will see that by Year 9 (the end of Key Stage 3) you should be at Level 5 or 6. The table includes the levels for 7-, 11- and 14-year-olds (for the end of Key Stages 1, 2 and 3) to give you an overall picture of the progress you should have made.

What you need to know about the National Tests

		Above	7 years	11 years	14 years
☐	Exceptional performance	Level 8			☐
		Level 8			▨
▨	Exceeded targets for age group	Level 7			▨
		Level 6		☐	☐
☐	Achieved targets for age group	Level 5		▨	☐
		Level 4	☐	☐	■
■	Working towards targets for age group	Level 3	▨	■	■
		Level 2	☐	■	■
		Level 1	■	■	■

Your achievements compared with other students

There are different National Tests papers for different ability levels. This is to ensure that students can take a test paper where they can show positive achievement. For English the tests are arranged in one group of levels. This group, known as a tier, covers Levels 4–7. The tier has two test papers, which will take $1\frac{1}{4} - 1\frac{1}{2}$ hours to complete. Extension test papers with high level questions can also be taken by exceptionally bright students. This book concentrates on Levels 4–7. The table below shows you what percentage of students nationally reached each of the levels in the 1995 tests for English.

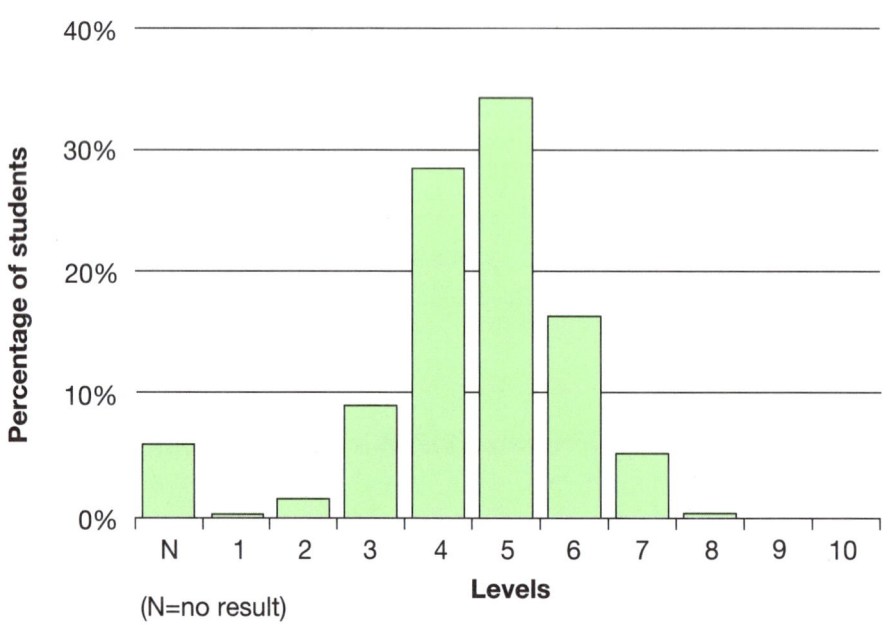

Levels achieved in English, 1995

Preparing and practising for the National Tests

ENGLISH AT KEY STAGE 3

The questions in this book will help you prepare by testing you on the Key Stage 3 curriculum for English. For assessment purposes, the National Curriculum divides English into three sections, called Attainment Targets (ATs). The first AT, Speaking and Listening, is assessed only by the teacher in the classroom, not in the written tests. The other two ATs are:
- AT2: Reading
- AT3: Writing

The English National Curriculum defines level descriptions for each of the ATs. These are taken together to give an overall level for English. The test papers have questions covering each of these ATs.

USING THIS BOOK TO HELP YOU PREPARE FOR THE NATIONAL TEST IN ENGLISH

This book contains three basic features:
- Questions: two test papers for Levels 4–7
- Answers: showing acceptable responses and marks, and advice from examiners on how to assess your work.
- Level chart: showing you how to interpret your marks to arrive at a level.

Details of how to do the tests at home are given below. Information about how to mark the tests and assess yourself can be found throughout the Answer section. Try to do Paper 1, mark the test and see how you do, and work through the advice given. Then, on a different day, try Paper 2.

Preparing and practising for the National Tests

SIMULATING TEST CONDITIONS
Paper 1 should take $1\frac{1}{2}$ hours and Paper 2 should take $1\frac{1}{4}$ hours. Carry out the tests in a place where you are comfortable. You will need a pencil, a ruler and a few sheets of A4 lined paper. If you have not finished after the set time carry on working until you finish.

If you do not understand a word you can ask an adult to explain what it means.

MARKING THE QUESTIONS
Guidance on how to mark your answers to the questions is given throughout the Answer section (Paper 1 pages 9-32; Paper 2 pages 33-50).

FINALLY, AS THE TESTS DRAW NEAR
In the days before the tests, make sure you are as relaxed and confident as possible. You can help yourself by:

- ensuring you know what test papers you will be doing and how to answer them

- looking back over any completed practice papers and making notes on key points to remember

- rereading your set Shakespeare play.

Above all, don't worry too much! So long as you have worked hard during the year and do your best in the tests, then that is all that anybody could ask.

Paper 1
Reading and writing

Instructions to student

Remember

- First of all, you have 15 minutes to read the paper. You may make notes and annotate the passages. Do not start to write your answers until told to do so.

- You then have 1 hour 30 minutes to write your answers.

- Answer **all** of the questions in Sections A and B, and **one** question only from Section C.

- You are advised to spend about 40–45 minutes on Section C.

- Your spelling and handwriting will be assessed in this paper.

- Check your work carefully.

This English test does not demand a particular number of words per question.

Using this practice paper, and following the instructions with regard to time and points to consider, will show you how much you are able to write.

The mark allocations per question will also help you to decide how much to write.

In the 15 minutes of reading time, you should first skim read in order to get a sense of the whole paper. Then read the passages, questions and assignments more carefully.

Remember effective reading and writing is dependent on **thinking** and (within the limits of a test situation) **planning**.

You may want to do some planning in the last five minutes of your reading time.

Paper 1
Reading and writing

Section A

Read the passage **Talking in Whispers** *which is in the pull-out section at the end of this book.*

Then answer Question 1 and Question 2.

Refer to words and phrases in the passage to support your ideas.

15 marks

1 In lines 1 to 58 Andres spots his friend Braulio and makes contact with an American photographer.

What do you learn about the situation, and Andres' reactions to it?

In your answer you should comment on:

- what happens to the prisoners;
- what Andres does;
- what Andres thinks and feels.

15 marks

2 Now look again at the section from line 59 to the end of the passage.

The danger of the situation increases. There is also a sense of hope.

How are the feelings of increasing danger and some hope built up?

In your answer you should comment on:

- the American photographer;
- the behaviour of the soldiers;
- Andres' reactions.

Paper 1
Reading and writing

Section B

Read the pamphlet reproduced in the pull-out section at the end of this book.

Amnesty International sends leaflets like this to people, asking them to become members.

Now answer Question 3.

3 **In what ways does this leaflet try to persuade people to join Amnesty International?** *20 marks*

In your answer you should comment on:

- the content and layout of the leaflet;
- why Amnesty International is needed;
- how and why Amnesty International is effective;
- how your joining up can help.

Paper 1
Reading and writing

Section C

*Choose **ONE** of the following.*

30 marks   **4**   EITHER

    a   **Write about a situation when you faced some danger – whether trivial or serious.**

- You could write about a real or imaginary experience.

OR

    b   You decide to form a Young Amnesty International group at your school – helping by raising money and joining in activities.

Write a letter to the parents of your year group, explaining what you plan to do.

You could include:

- reasons why you want to support this cause;

- activities you are hoping to organise;

- ways of raising money to support Amnesty International;

- how you want parents to support your activities.

- You do not need to write an address. Begin your letter by writing: Dear Parents,

Paper 2
Shakespeare Play

Instructions to student

Remember

- The test is 1 hour 15 minues long.

- You should do the task from **one** of the following plays:

Romeo and Juliet

Julius Caesar

A Midsummer Night's Dream

In the pull-out section at the back of this book you will find the relevant text from whichever play you choose.

- Your work will be assessed for your knowledge and understanding of the play and the way you express your ideas. Your spelling and handwriting will also be assessed.

- You will gain extra credit if you:
  – use details and quotations from the scene to support your ideas;
  – comment on the language of the characters;
  – refer to other parts of the play when they fit in with your answer.

- Check your work carefully.

Paper 2
Shakespeare Play

EITHER

Romeo and Juliet
Act 3 Scene 3, Lines 1–175

40 marks

Task 1

In this scene there is desperation and other extreme moods. There is also coolness and reason and even some admiration.

Show where these occur. Explain how they might affect the audience's feelings about Friar Lawrence at this point in the play.

Before you begin to write you should think about:

- Romeo's state of mind at the start of the scene;

- Romeo's state of mind at the end of the scene;

- What the Friar says to Romeo;

- What the Nurse says to the Friar.

Paper 2
Shakespeare Play

OR

Julius Caesar
Act 3 Scene 2, Lines 1–221

Task 2

You are one of the Plebians listening and reacting to the speeches of Brutus and Mark Antony.

40 marks

Explain what Brutus and Mark Antony have to say and its effect on you. Your mood will change during the scene. Explain why.

Before you begin to write you should think about:

- what happened before this scene and what happens after it;

- the ways in which your feelings change as you listen;

- the words Brutus uses to justify his actions;

- the ways in which Mark Antony sways the people listening with you;

- the different views of Brutus and Antony about Caesar's death.

Paper 2
Shakespeare Play

OR

A Midsummer Night's Dream
Act 4 Scene 1, Lines 43–211

40 marks

Task 3

This scene shows how the arguments and misunderstandings between the characters come to an end.

Think about Titania, Demetrius and Bottom. Does this scene make you believe that everything is sorted out for them?

Give reasons for what you think based on what the characters say and do in the scene.

Before you begin to write you should think about:

- the way Oberon and Titania settle their quarrel;

- what Demetrius says about his experiences;

- what Bottom says when he wakes up;

- the language the characters use to express their thoughts and feelings;

- whether you think that this scene ends happily for Titania, Demetrius and Bottom.

Paper 1 Answers

As in every test situation it is important to think your answers through.

Answers to Questions 1, 2 and 3 will all benefit from both thorough and skim reading. Do not be afraid to make notes on the text, underlining key words or features or circling relevant sentences or phrases.

You will have had many opportunities throughout KS2 to demonstrate your reading and writing skills. Many of these would have involved the drafting and redrafting of your answers.

A test offers a very limited scope for you to show your writing skills. Obviously time pressures are a factor with which you have to contend, and which mirror problems you may have later in life when working to deadlines. The test is intended to confirm the decisions your teacher has made about the quality of your work.

The best you can hope for is to begin to develop an understanding of the central aspects of the skills you have been taught and some grasp of the Writing Assessment Criteria (see pages 16-17) being used to measure your test achievements. This is a set of criteria designed to enable you to have some idea of the level and marks your answers to Paper 1 would be likely to gain. Read them and consider their application.

On pages 18, 21 and 23 these criteria have been applied to Ben's answers to Questions 1, 2 and 3.

On pages 26 and 30 these criteria have been applied to Carrie's writing about the flood and Aimee's writing about raising money for Amnesty International.

The pages which follow take you through several stages of assessing your performance. You are:

- reminded of the task;
- given pointers about what to include in your answer;
- provided with assessment criteria for gauging the quality of your work;
- shown sample answers by other students;
- supplied with detailed comments on those answers.

Paper 1 Answers

Section A   Question 1

You will find the question on page 2.

REMINDER OF THE TASK
In lines 1–58 of *Talking in Whispers*, Andres spots his friend Braulio and makes contact with an American photographer.

What do you learn about the situation and Andres' reaction to it?

In your answer you should comment on:

- what happens to the prisoners;
- what Andres does;
- what Andres thinks and feels.

You are being asked to:

- read closely, attending to detail and overall meaning, showing the ability to read with insight;
- select material appropriate to the purpose;
- sustain and develop interpretations of the text, supporting opinion by references to the text.

KEY POINTS
Your answer could refer to some of the following key points:

What happens to the prisoners	What Andres does	What Andres thinks and feels
• the prisoners are beaten if they hesitate to leave the trucks;	• stays clear of the crowd;	• he is desperate to get through the crowd;
• Andres' friend jumps from the truck;	• watches the truck arrive;	• he forgets his own danger;
• the last prisoners are driven from the truck;	• sees his friend;	• is afraid the American has a gun;
• the guards beat one who is too slow.	• breaks forward, seeking a gap;	• feels a thrill of hope about the presence of a pressman;
	• follows the American;	• he forgets his own danger out of concern for his friend, Braulio.
	• tells him the world's got to know;	
	• gets the crowd to part;	
	• accepts his camera.	

NOTE
Good answers will show empathy with the characters and support for your insights. Inferences will be drawn from evidence in the text. They will show the development in Andres' reactions to the changing situation. Keep your mind on the lead question and link your answers to this.

Paper 1 Answers

Section A   Question 2

You will find the question on page 2.

REMINDER OF THE TASK
Now look again at the section from line 59 to the end of the passage.

The danger of the situation increases. There is also a sense of hope.

How are your feelings of increasing danger and some hope built up?

In your answer you should comment on:

- the American photographer;
- the behaviour of the soldiers;
- Andres' reactions.

You are being asked to:

- show engagement with the ideas and theme of the extract;
- show understanding of how the writer uses structural devices to achieve effect;
- sustain and develop interpretations of the text, supporting opinions by references to the text.

KEY POINTS
Your answer could refer to some of the following key points:

The American photographer	The behaviour of the soldiers	Andres' reactions
• he cannot be saved by the crowd;	• their beating of the American photographer;	• initially a helpless onlooker;
• he is a victim of violence (answers may refer to how this is conveyed);	• their search for the camera;	• overcome by the strength of the Junta;
• the soldiers are searching for his camera;	• their flinging of Don Chailey, the American photographer, out of the Stadium.	• realisation that the film is an important proof of the Junta's brutality;
• he is an American citizen (answers may develop the significance of this).		• witness of brutality to an American citizen;
		• new found sense of purpose.

NOTE
Do not just list the events. Try to show how the feeling of danger increases and how a sense of hope develops. Link your answer to the lead question.

11

Paper 1 Answers

Section B   Question 3

You will find the question on page 3.

REMINDER OF THE TASK
Read the Amnesty International leaflet.

In what ways does this leaflet try to persuade people to join Amnesty International?

In your answer you are being asked to:

- distinguish between fact and opinion;
- follow the thread of an argument, identifying and recognising any inconsistencies;
- show understanding of how a writer uses language and presentation to achieve effect.

KEY POINTS
Your answer could refer to some of the following key points:

Content and layout

- direct and urgent tone: something has to be done;
- use of bold, direct headlines beginning with a direct quotation which leads the reader to wish to know more;
- graphic photographs, effect of violence;
- short factual paragraphs combined with dramatic language e.g. 'sickening abuse' 'didn't have real hope', 'brutal injustices';
- use of current cases and letters from former prisoners and their families;
- reader involved as someone with potential to help;
- illustration of pen waiting to be used.

Why Amnesty International is needed

- 'prisoners of conscience': imprisoned, unfairly tried, tortured, executed because of who they are or what they believe;
- scale of the problem;
- particular individual examples;
- scores of governments involved;
- 43,500 individuals campaigned for since 1961.

How and why Amnesty International is effective

- brings concerned individuals together;
- spans all political, religious, ethnic and age groups;
- independent of governments;
- puts pressure on governments;
- highlights injustices;
- publishes facts on torture and unfair imprisonment;
- asks questions of governments;
- organises letter writing campaigns.

How your joining Amnesty International can help

- it gives hope to the prisoners;
- it makes them feel less isolated;
- donations help funding;
- adds your voice to others around the world.

NOTE
Good answers will show a grasp of the persuasive arguments and comment on how pictures, presentation and the choice of language add to the impact to the leaflet.

Paper 1 Answers

Section C Question 4a

You will find the question on page 4.

REMINDER OF THE TASK
Write about a situation when you faced some danger – whether trivial or serious.

- You could write about a real or imaginary experience.

In your answer you could include:

- how the dangerous situation developed: did the danger occur suddenly or did it come about gradually?
- how you felt at different stages of the occasion;
- dramatic recreation of the moments of danger;
- significant details of the place, people and events in the situation;
- how the situation was resolved – if at all.

In your answer you are being asked to:

- show that you can present content so as to engage and sustain the interest of the reader;
- structure sequences of events and ideas in ways that make meaning clear to a reader;
- sustain a chosen style;
- write accurately.

ADVICE TO STUDENTS
The chances of creating a successful response to this type of task can be improved if you:

- **plan your writing;**
- choose a subject or setting with which you have some familiarity;
- centre your writing around a simple plot;
- begin with a dramatic opening;
- vary the pace and focus on a small number of characters and a single setting;
- explore the emotions and feelings of the main characters;
- use interesting and varied language, including some dialogue to convey character, settings and feelings;
- try to end with some sort of self-knowledge or high/low points.

Paper 1 Answers

KEY POINTS
Answers could refer to some of the following key points:

- aim for a strong beginning and a clear, shaped ending;
- paragraph your writing to indicate the main elements and turning points in the structure;
- vary your sentence structure;
- use a wide range of vocabulary;
- include detail to bring the writing alive;
- check your writing for spelling and punctuation.

NOTE
A well-structured piece of writing will be more successful than a longer rambling one.

Paper 1 Answers

Section C   Question 4b

You will find the question on page 4.

REMINDER OF THE TASK
You decide to form a Young Amnesty International group at your school – helping by raising money and joining in activities.

Write a letter to the parents of your year group, explaining what you plan to do.

In your answer you are being asked to:

- show that you can present content so as to engage and sustain the interest of the reader;
- structure sequences of events and ideas in ways that make the meaning clear to a reader;
- inform and persuade a specific audience;
- sustain a chosen style;
- write accurately.

KEY POINTS
Your answer could refer to some of the following key points:

- reasons why you want to support this cause;
- activities you are hoping to organise;
- ways of raising money to support Amnesty International;
- assuring parents that this is a good course of action;
- how you want parents to support your activities.

NOTE
Responding successfully to this question involves clarity of thought, and persuasion of the reader. It should appeal to logic and emotion and a sense of involvement.

Paper 1 Answers

How to assess and improve your own writing

The writing assessment criteria that follow will enable you to judge the National Curriculum level at which your writing may be placed. It should be stressed that these criteria are a *guide*. They will be of most use to you as a way of looking for, and developing, these qualities in your own writing.

Look back at your answers in the light of these criteria. Give yourself a mark, up to a maximum of 6 within each level, for each point included in your response. What level have you reached? If you get 6 marks or below you are working at Level 3.

Fill in your marks on the chart on page 51.

WRITING ASSESSMENT CRITERIA

Marks 7–12

LEVEL 4
- The reader is led from one event/idea to the next with understanding and interest, making them clear to the reader.
- Subject matter is substantially relevant to the task, arranged in an orderly way – making ideas clear to the reader, using appropriate detail.
- If appropriate, there is indication of appearance/motive/feeling with added description and/or information conveyed; opinion is expressed.
- Simple sentences are written correctly.
- More complicated structures are present; paragraphing may be present.
- The vocabulary is used effectively.
- Spelling, including that of polysyllabic words that conform to regular patterns, is generally accurate.
- Handwriting style is fluent, joined and legible.

Marks 13–18

LEVEL 5
- The reader's interest is engaged through the writer's clear, accessible, structured approach.
- Subject matter is clearly relevant, events or ideas are easily followed.
- When appropriate there is simple characterisation and setting, descriptive detail, a developed line of argument.
- Sentences may be mainly simple but more complex structures are attempted.
- Sentences are usually correctly punctuated. If appropriate, attempts are made to punctuate direct speech and other marks (?!) are used on some appropriate occasions. Paragraphs are used with understanding of their function and interrelationship.
- Vocabulary is large enough to fulfil the task with some more colourful description or use of language to 'force' an opinion. There may be some figurative language (e.g. metaphors or similes).
- Words with complex regular patterns are usually spelt correctly.
- Handwriting is joined, clear and fluent and, where appropriate, adapted to a range of tasks.

Paper 1 Answers

		Marks 9–24
LEVEL 6	• Life and movement hold the reader's interest – with, at times, a definite awareness of the reader.	
	• Meaning is consistently clear.	
	• Ideas and information are developed. When appropriate there is development of character and description, with original observation and variety. When views are expressed there is an element of logic and development of ideas.	
	• There will be some variety of sentence length and type attempted, possibly with experimentation with word order for effect.	
	• Common forms of punctuation, including direct speech, are used accurately. Sentence joins are correct. Paragraphs organise ideas of events.	
	• More complex language is attempted – vocabulary is used to achieve particular effects. Style may be varied to suit the task with some figurative language if appropriate (e.g. metaphors or similes).	
	• Spelling is generally accurate, including that of irregular words.	
	• Handwriting is neat and legible.	

		Marks 25–30
LEVEL 7	• The style is confident and appropriately written with shape and purpose aimed at sustaining the reader's interest.	
	• The piece appears to have been given shape and purpose with an audience's needs in mind.	
	• Story features are confidently handled with good observation, sensitivity and description. Views are effectively stated with some coherence.	
	• Sentences are varied, occasionally complex and accurately constructed and used.	
	• Accurate, helpful punctuation makes ideas or events clear to the reader. Paragraphs are used, with some linking.	
	• There is a range of appropriate effective vocabulary – with successful attempts at figurative language if appropriate and/or some rhetorical devices.	
	• Spelling is correct, including that of complex irregular words.	
	• Work is legible and attractively presented.	

Paper 1
Sample answers

> **Section A   Question 1**

The criteria that follow are specific to your answers to the passage from *Talking in Whispers*, Question 1.

Use them to look back at your answer. Identify the qualities in your answer that are listed here, and note the qualities you need to work on to improve your performance.

ASSESSMENT CRITERIA

LEVEL 4
- There may be a little explanation – showing some understanding of the main ideas. The answer is mostly relevant, selecting facts and narrative which are occasionally relevant to the question. There will be a few points with brief explanations, e.g. 'looks for his friend'.

LEVEL 5
- A fuller answer with linked explanations, showing more detailed understanding. Competent, quite wide-ranging answers cover the more obvious points. For example, they may explain the situation of the prisoners and provide some details of what Andres does.

LEVEL 6
- A better developed answer with some explanation. Points are sometimes developed in detail. There is evidence of insight and involvement in seeing the situation from Andres' point of view. Relevant generalisations are made, e.g. 'Andres was feeling desperate'. There is a beginning of understanding of what was behind Andres' concern. There may be some explanation of the changes in his behaviour, thoughts or feelings. An answer at this level will be sustained by reference to the text and will relate the detail of what is happening to his thoughts and feelings.

LEVEL 7
- A good, reasonably full answer showing understanding of the text as a whole and closely linked to it. Answers show a clear grasp of more complex ideas such as the importance of the photographic evidence of brutality and the details of the text which convey this idea. An overview is taken and different parts of the answer are linked. Comments on the behaviour of other people are made relevant to Andres' reactions.

Paper 1 Sample answers

Ben's answer

Consider this answer to Question 1, written by Ben, a Year 9 student. His errors have been corrected. What level would you give it? Refer back to the specific criteria opposite.

You will find the question on page 2.

Talking In Whispers

The situation in which Andres finds himself is clearly so confused and chaotic that his feelings seem to change in each paragraph. The crowds on the road to the stadium are both familiar – like the crowds on match day – and yet strange since in fact they are either prisoners, soldiers or ordinary people who are looking for their captured and/or missing friends, a situation far from everyday life though, the writer implies, one which is becoming gradually more commonplace for the people of marshall law Chile. The confusion of this situation is shown in the confusion of the language – the second paragraph is full of incomplete lists and unfinished questions. This, then, in turn reflects Andres' own confusion. When he considers the loss of his other friends he feels hopeless – how can he alone combat the might of the whole army. Yet the example of his friends and their resistance reminds him of the example of David and Goliath and fills him with new hope. Similarly, when he sees Braulio, looking battered but unbowed, the example makes him forget the danger he is himself in and push forward to help his friend. His responses to the arrival of Don Chailey also veer from fear that the American is armed and will attract danger to a near jubilation that an outsider is coming to aid the resistance and record the atrocities that are going on. Since the passage is written largely from Andres' perspective it allows us to see the way in which his feelings chaotically mirror the chaos around him, and serves to suggest the way in which danger and exhaustion heighten emotional response.

Assessment of Ben's answer

Compare Ben's answer to the key points on page 10.

- He presents his ideas very confidently.
- He sets about answering the tasks quickly.
- He makes many relevant references to the extract.
- He is able to keep control of long sentences containing a number of ideas. For example, 'Since the passage is written largely from Andres' perspective it allows us to see the way in which his feelings chaotically mirror the chaos around him and serves to suggest the way in which danger and exhaustion heighten emotional response.'
- Despite the pressures of time, in his actual test answer Ben's handwriting is clear and his spelling and punctuation are mainly correct.

Paper 1
Sample answers

- Ideas are clearly connected using words such as 'though', 'this', 'then', 'yet', 'when', 'similarly', 'since'.
- He doesn't simply retell the events of the passages.

Ben's piece seems to merit a Level 7 mark. He refers closely to the text, is sensitive to its inferences, has a clear grasp of complex ideas and links different parts of his answer to each other. Furthermore, he is aware of the way in which language is used to create effect.

Paper 1
Sample answers

Section A   Question 2

Again, the criteria that follow are specific to your answers to the passage from *Talking in Whispers*. This time they refer to Question 2.

Use them to look back at your answer. Identify the qualities in your answer that are listed here, and note the qualities you need to work on to improve your performance.

ASSESSMENT CRITERIA

LEVEL 4
- A little explanation, showing some understanding. There will be *some* summary of the sources of danger and hope, for example a statement about the beating or the search for the camera. There may be some reference to Andres' trembling. There may be some grasp of the importance of the film.

LEVEL 5
- There will be some explanations, a number of points without much detail and a fuller understanding of the text. The danger may be mentioned without much detail, so might the sense of hope – without a full explanation. The answer will be built into a sequence of linked events.

LEVEL 6
- This will be better developed, with some exploration of the text; points will sometimes be developed in detail. There will be an appreciation of how the writer introduces some hope. There may be explanation of how the violence is conveyed or understanding of how Andres would feel. The answer will be supported by reference to the text.

LEVEL 7
- A good answer shows a clearly expressed understanding of the whole text and is closely linked to it, in a detailed way, through reference or relevant quotations. There is an understanding of *how* the writer conveys the danger and the feelings of hope. The answer may identify the moment when everything changes, comment on the depiction of Andres' feelings and show how the events lead to an optimistic climax.

Paper 1 Sample answers

Ben's answer

Now consider this answer to Question 2, also written by Ben. Ben's errors have been corrected. What level would you give it? Refer to the assessment criteria on page 21.

You will find the question on page 2.

The American photographer stands out in more ways than one. Just as he is a focus of hope for Andres he is clearly the focus of anger for the soldiers. At first Andres is relieved that Don is not carrying a gun but – as he points out at the end of the passage – in many respects a camera is just as dangerous as a gun in this situation. The soldiers are shown as a solid presence amidst the confusion because they have the force to beat their way through the crowd. Suddenly Andres is not just another nameless person – the camera which causes the death of Don Chailey is passed on to him.

i.e. identifies Andres with Don (shows the result of Don putting himself in a dangerous position)

Assessment of Ben's answer

Ben's answer to Question 2, although briefer, concentrates on the key words of the question - 'danger' and 'hope'. Check his answer against the key points on page 11.

Ben refers economically to a number of important points. He does not get drawn into long repetition of the text, choosing instead to give an overview of the important points.

- He recognises the significance of the American photographer and his camera.
- He show how Andres' reactions change.
- He recognises the contract between the power of the soldiers and the confusion amongst the people.

Ben's answer to Question 2 is not quite as good as his answer to Question 1, though he does show an understanding of the significance of the passage. There is appreciation of the passage as a whole and some reference to the text, though the approach is not as detailed as in his first answer. What is missing is a finer attention to detail and the language of the passage. A Level 6 would be appropriate.

Paper 1
Sample answers

Section B   Question 3

The following assessment criteria refer to the Amnesty International material.

Use them to look back at your answer. Identify the qualities in your answer that are listed here, and note the qualities you need to work on to improve your performance.

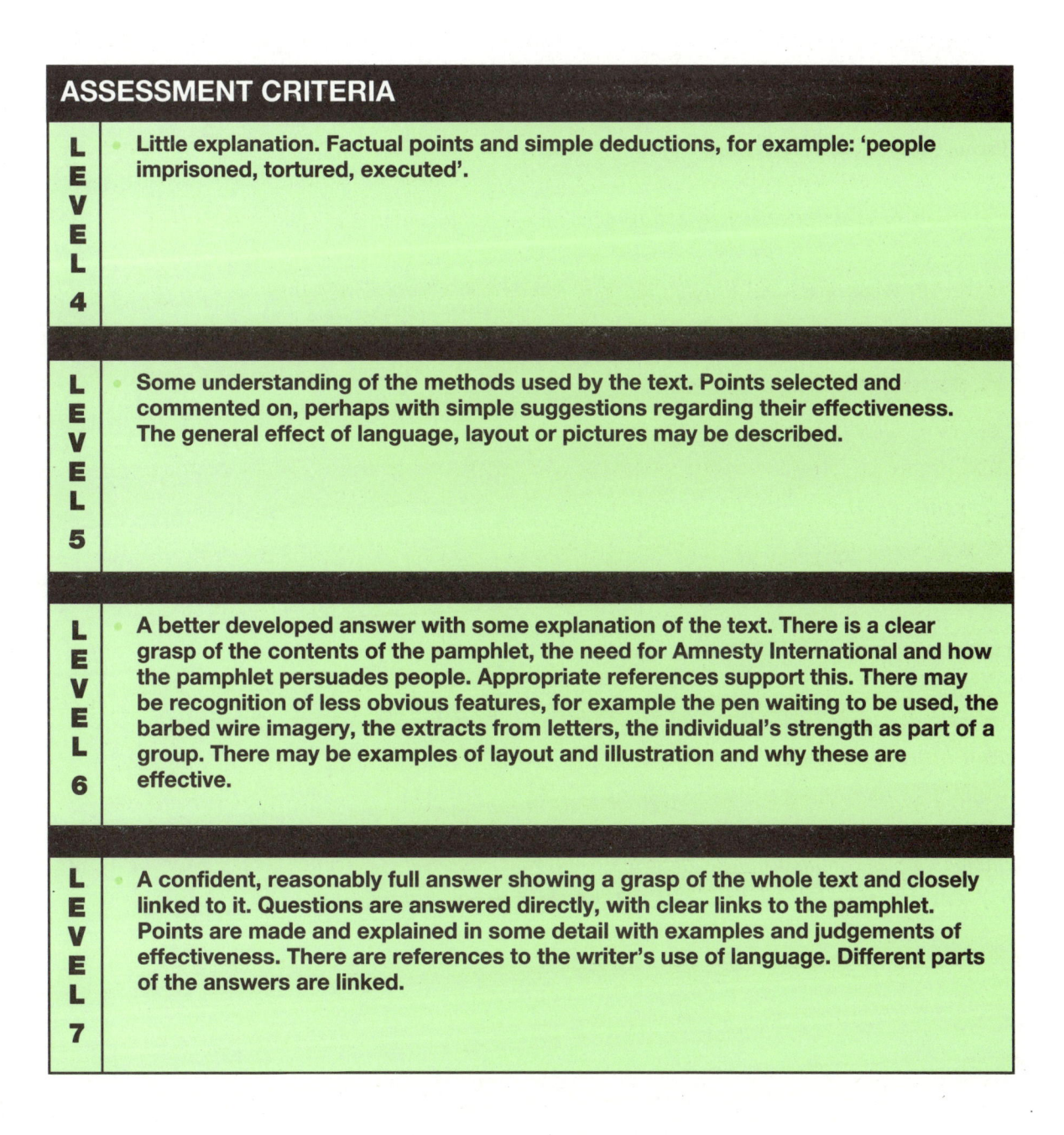

ASSESSMENT CRITERIA

LEVEL 4
- Little explanation. Factual points and simple deductions, for example: 'people imprisoned, tortured, executed'.

LEVEL 5
- Some understanding of the methods used by the text. Points selected and commented on, perhaps with simple suggestions regarding their effectiveness. The general effect of language, layout or pictures may be described.

LEVEL 6
- A better developed answer with some explanation of the text. There is a clear grasp of the contents of the pamphlet, the need for Amnesty International and how the pamphlet persuades people. Appropriate references support this. There may be recognition of less obvious features, for example the pen waiting to be used, the barbed wire imagery, the extracts from letters, the individual's strength as part of a group. There may be examples of layout and illustration and why these are effective.

LEVEL 7
- A confident, reasonably full answer showing a grasp of the whole text and closely linked to it. Questions are answered directly, with clear links to the pamphlet. Points are made and explained in some detail with examples and judgements of effectiveness. There are references to the writer's use of language. Different parts of the answers are linked.

Paper 1 Sample answers

Ben's answer

Here is Ben's answer to Question 3. Ben's errors have been corrected. Refer back to the specific criteria on page 23 and decide at what level you would place this answer.

You will find the question on page 3.

Apparently very factual – lots of specific examples detailing cases, basic description of circumstances, not detailed description of torture/abduction/horror.

Because it states the cases so simply it gets you on side.

3 parts: 1 factual description of real people ∴ human rights abuses are real.

    2 Work of AI and finally what you can do.

    3 Letters ie what result of you joining would be

    ∴ well structured.

Impression of AI

AI – reasonable, calm organisation getting on with its mandate, non political, no axe to grind.

picture of suffering in middle, then solution at the bottom – the pen.

This is structure of first 2 parts of the leaflet too – the rights abuse cases = question, the AI & what they do = answer).

= reason to join – see how it changes people's lives, how grateful they are. – shows how you can change the world, and although these are real letters from real people, not made up for the advert, but genuine, they give out a sense of elation which passes on to the reader.

Paper 1
Sample answers

Assessment of Ben's answer

Ben's answer to Section B, Question 3 is direct and to the point. Although in his actual written answer his presentation is less than his best this is acceptable given the pressures of time in this test situation. He conveys a clear understanding of the question and the language content, ideas, structure and persuasive techniques of the leaflet.

Here is a more detailed assessment of Ben's answer:

- he has paid only a little attention to layout and illustration.
- he has identified the structure and overall layout of the pamphlet, but although he suggests it is 'well structured', he doesn't say why;
- the list-like nature of his answer does not allow him to develop ideas;
- it's not certain that the letters quoted *are* real;
- he has focussed well on the tone of the pamphlet: its calm, measured persuasiveness;
- there isn't as much detailed reference to the material as there might be;
- he could have made more of the links between the images and the words.

His overall performance on this question merits a mark at the top of the Level 5 range. Do you agree?

Paper 1
Sample answers

Section C   Question 4a

The criteria that follow are specific to the writing task in Question 4a, 'Write about a situation when you faced some danger – whether trivial or serious.'

Use them to assess your own writing first. Then look at Carrie's answer in the light of them.

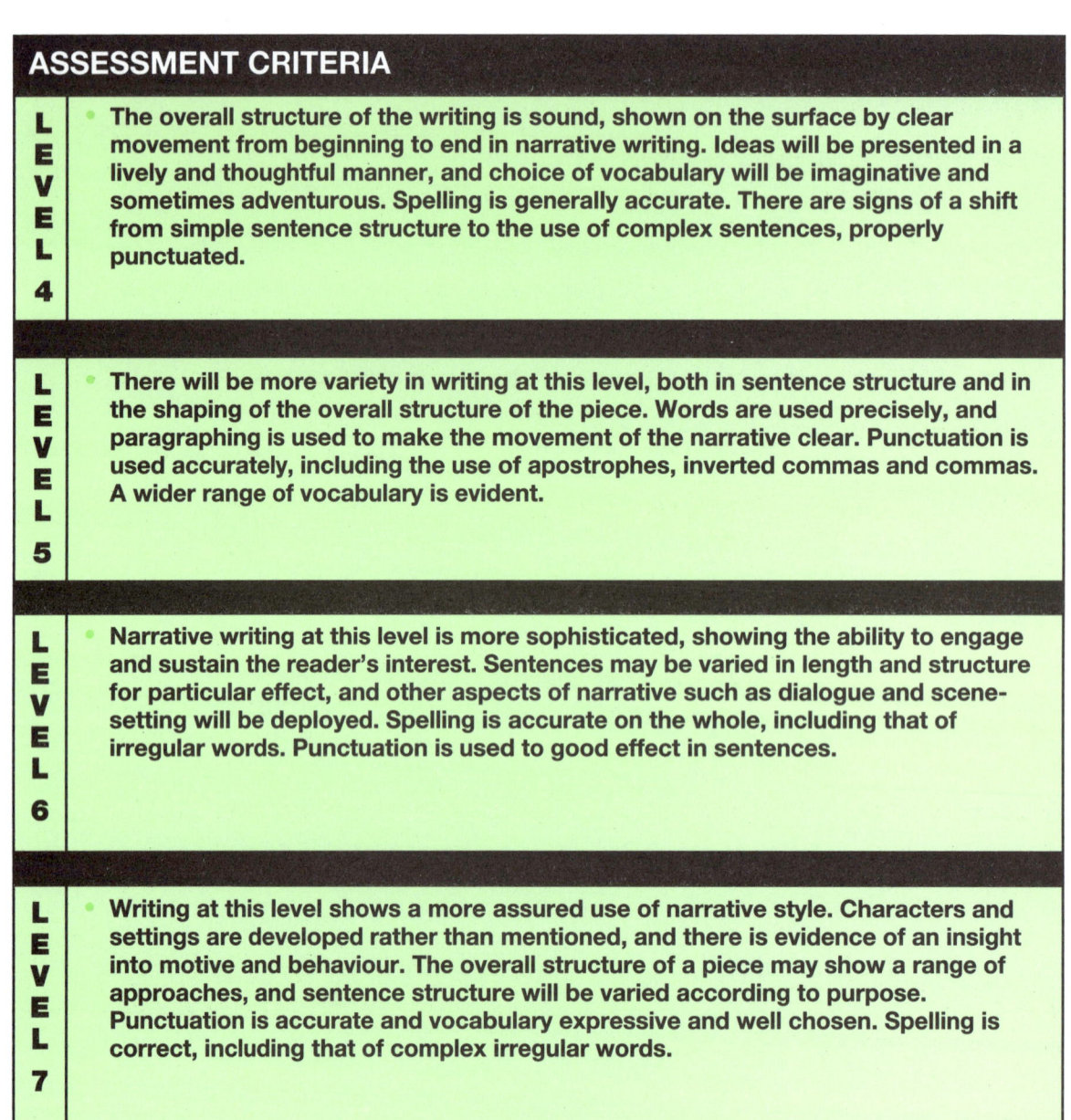

ASSESSMENT CRITERIA

LEVEL 4
- The overall structure of the writing is sound, shown on the surface by clear movement from beginning to end in narrative writing. Ideas will be presented in a lively and thoughtful manner, and choice of vocabulary will be imaginative and sometimes adventurous. Spelling is generally accurate. There are signs of a shift from simple sentence structure to the use of complex sentences, properly punctuated.

LEVEL 5
- There will be more variety in writing at this level, both in sentence structure and in the shaping of the overall structure of the piece. Words are used precisely, and paragraphing is used to make the movement of the narrative clear. Punctuation is used accurately, including the use of apostrophes, inverted commas and commas. A wider range of vocabulary is evident.

LEVEL 6
- Narrative writing at this level is more sophisticated, showing the ability to engage and sustain the reader's interest. Sentences may be varied in length and structure for particular effect, and other aspects of narrative such as dialogue and scene-setting will be deployed. Spelling is accurate on the whole, including that of irregular words. Punctuation is used to good effect in sentences.

LEVEL 7
- Writing at this level shows a more assured use of narrative style. Characters and settings are developed rather than mentioned, and there is evidence of an insight into motive and behaviour. The overall structure of a piece may show a range of approaches, and sentence structure will be varied according to purpose. Punctuation is accurate and vocabulary expressive and well chosen. Spelling is correct, including that of complex irregular words.

Paper 1
Sample answers

Carrie's answer

Read Carrie's answer to Question 4a. Since her answer is being assessed on Writing rather than Reading, any errors have been retained. What level do you think it would be? Refer to the specific criteria opposite.

You will find the question on page 4.

We'd been living in the valley for about 8 years before it happened. The old barn had been completely rebuilt by my parents, using local materials and craftsmen. As a family we had been happy to leave Birmingham and make a new life in the west of Wales. Mums job as a translator could be easily done from home and Dad was happy with our fields and sheep, and restoring old furniture.

Everything was fine. The locals were friendly and it had been fun to learn Welsh in school.

Yes, everything was fine until that spring morning. The tides were unusually high, the rainfall was unending.

It came on the news but we already knew. This would be the last night that anyone in our village would be able to stay in their own homes. The constant torrents of heavy rain had caused the river to rise ever-higher, the danger ever closer.

It was at a point that was maybe eight hours before it broke through the barriers, but the way it was rising, it seemed like it wouldn't last four, yet alone eight. Mum decided that we wouldn't risk staying.

All our most precious belongings had been stored upstairs. We prayed that those would be safe – we knew no-one local would loot them, and hoped no strangers would be around. It seemed unlikely, given the weather!

Dad had the Land Rover running as we crammed ourselves, the two dogs, sleeping bags and spare clothing into the back. The sheep and early lambs had been taken to temporary barns further up the valley sides. Dad was torn between driving us to safety and staying with them.

Safety! We still had to travel along the road by the foaming torrents that formed the once placid Dovey river. Visibility was down to the minimum, the faster the wipers moved the more the rain seemed to block our view of what might lay ahead.

Paper 1 Sample answers

Our progress seemed painfully slow – he kept to the crest of where he thought the road may be, along the valley towards the tiny church at the top of the hill.

Dad knew he must keep the motor running. Fortunately this ex-Army Land-Rover had a vertical exhaust, but it was still touch and go. None of the children spoke – leaving him to drive & Mum to 'navigate'.

'We should have bought a boat,' he muttered.

Soon the worst was over. The church like a beacon, called us ever closer to its welcome light. It had been specially opened up for all who lived on the river banks, a refuge in case the barriers should burst and flood our homes.

By morning the church was crammed full. The river had flooded most of the village and we were marooned on this hilltop. I thought of our barn and how eight years work would now be ruined, the belongings we hadn't been able to move floating around.

Ours was a strong community. People shared any food they had brought, calor gas heaters added to the radiators of the church.

We had faced danger and survived!

Assessment of Carrie's answer

Notice that Carrie has chosen to use the title to write on a topic about which, presumably, she feels able to display knowledge, talent and interest. Do feel free to use the titles set in the test to produce writing with which you feel comfortable.

Use these criteria to ask yourself questions about her story. For example:

- Is it confidently written?
- Does it have some shape?
- Is your interest sustained?
- Identify particular story features – what is observed? How is description used? Circle or underline particular features.
- Check the range of sentences, including variations in length or structure. Do they make the story more effective?
- How does Carrie use punctuation? Make up headlines for each paragraph – how 'independent' are they and how are they connected?

Paper 1
Sample answers

Now think of the overall impression made by the story and, remembering that Carrie produced her story in test conditions, decide on a level for it.

Carrie's answer to Question 4a achieves a Level 7 for a number of reasons:

- she shows a confident, assured style;
- the drama is well developed, building up from the calm, stable setting 'until that spring morning';
- character is not only well depicted at the start, but is developed throughout the piece;
- there is a strong sense of the nature of community and of the subtle differences between life in Birmingham and life in the Welsh countryside;
- the writing is well paragraphed – on the whole they are short, but dialogue is correctly presented and the momentum of the narrative is well served by the paragraphing;
- punctuation is largely accurate – there is use of complex, compound and simple sentence structure, all well punctuated;
- spelling is accurate;
- vocabulary is well chosen, ranging from the formal ('visibility was down to the minimum') to the colloquial ('the church was crammed full') in a natural, seemingly effortless way;
- there is variation in narrative voice: 'Yes, everything was fine...' as well as the standard third person narration.

Paper 1
Sample answers

Section C   Question 4b

The following criteria are specific to the writing task in Question 4b, 'Write a letter to the parents of your year group, explaining what you plan to do [in forming a Young Amnesty International group at your school]'.

Use them to assess your own writing first. Then look at Aimee's answer in the light of them.

ASSESSMENT CRITERIA

LEVEL 4
- The overall structure of the writing is sound, shown by a clear sequence in the setting out of ideas and the beginnings of a persuasive case. It is likely, though, that an argument will appear either unsubstantiated or as explanation. Ideas will be presented in a lively and thoughtful manner, and choice of vocabulary will be appropriate. Spelling is generally accurate. There are signs of a shift from simple sentence structure to the use of complex sentences, properly punctuated. Handwriting style is fluent, joined and legible.

LEVEL 5
- There will be more variety in writing at this level, both in sentence structure and in the shaping of the overall structure of the piece. Words are used precisely, and paragraphing is used to make the movement of the persuasive argument clear. Punctuation is used accurately, including the use of apostrophes, inverted commas and commas. A wider range of vocabulary is evident. Handwriting is fluent and, where appropriate, adapted to a range of functions.

LEVEL 6
- Informative and argumentative writing at this level is more sophisticated, showing the ability to engage and sustain the reader's interest. Sentences may be varied in length and structure for particular effect, and other aspects of non-fictional writing like analysis, clear layout and reflection will be deployed. Spelling is accurate on the whole, including that of irregular words. Handwriting is neat and legible. Punctuation is used to good effect in sentences.

LEVEL 7
- Writing at this level shows a more assured use of expository or argumentative style. The sense of audience will be clear, and the use of various devices to make a case or set out the nature of a case will be evident, for example anticipating objections to an argument. The overall structure of a piece may show a range of approaches, and sentence structure will be varied according to purpose. Punctuation is accurate and vocabulary expressive and well chosen. Spelling is correct, including that of complex irregular words. Work is legible and attractively presented.

Paper 1
Sample answers

Aimee's answer

Now read an answer to Question 4b by Aimee, a Year 9 student, reproduced here in her actual handwriting. What level do you think it would attain? Refer to the specific criteria opposite.

You will find the question on page 4.

> Dear Parents,
>
> We have decided to form a Young Amnesty International group to try and help people from all over the world who are victims of cruel governments.
>
> Our main reason is to raise money to support Amnesty and to form a letter writing group. If lots of individuals from all over the world who are writing to governments who torture people and put them in prison for their views then the governments might take notice, the prisoners will not feel forgotten.
>
> We hope to organise a number of activities :- Cluedo (the life size version), a talent contest and various sponsored events to raise money for our group.
>
> Quite a number of our year group are planning to raise money. One girl is being sponsored to try and conquer her fear of snakes by sitting for two hours with a snake around her neck! We are also holding a car wash day. We hope that you will sponsor some of the events arranged and come to have your car washed.
>
> The problem of political prisoners exists all around the world. Amnesty is in desperate need of funds and supporters and deserves your help. I know that there are a lot of deserving causes but I think that this is a chance for us to help suffering people around the world
>
> Not only will you and ourselves be

Paper 1 Sample answers

> raising money, we will be actively involved in letter writing. You are welcome to join us - assisting in our events, and if you would like to, writing letters.
> The 'Cluedo' event is on the 12th of May, the snake sit in takes place on the same day.
> A sponsor form is attatched.
> Thank you in advance for your co-operation
> Yours sincerely,
> Aimee Burrows

Assessment of Aimee's answer

This is an interesting letter. We learn about Amnesty, fundraising and how the reader can be involved. The reader's interest is sustained by her approach. Particular aspects are:

- Some planning has gone on – the clear structure is designed to achieve the purposes outlined in the question.

- A short introductory paragraph states the letter's purpose. The second paragraph summarises the work of Amnesty. Paragraphs three and four explain the fundraising activities. Paragraph five underlines and personalises the need for such an organisation. Paragraph six also aims to involve the reader. Necessary factual information is given in the remaining paragraphs.

- Aimee has used a range of persuasive phrases which have an emotional impact, for example 'cruel governments', 'who torture people', 'suffering people'.

- She meets people's objections to the singling out of Amnesty as an object for their charity, building up a sense of personal involvement and a sense of people acting together, for example 'people working together', 'a chance for us to help', 'actively involved', 'welcome to join us'.

- She puts her views forward with clarity and coherence. Her sentences show variety. They often contain more than one idea when this is appropriate and are easy to understand. There is a range of punctuation, helpfully and accurately used.

- Whenever it is appropriate each paragraph refers back to and develops what has gone before. There are a number of appealing sentences. She seems to be very able to use a range of vocabulary which is appropriate for her purposes.

- Handwriting and spellings produced under examination conditions cannot be expected to be anyone's best. Aimee's spelling (including irregular words except for 'attached') is generally accurate. Her work is neat and legible.

Such achievements would be likely to receive a mark within the Level 7 range.

Paper 2 Answers

As with Paper 1, it is important to think through your answer.

In the case of the Shakespeare paper, you are faced with a long passage from the play you have chosen to study and a single assignment you have to complete. You should choose the test paper for the play you have studied: *Romeo and Juliet* or *Julius Caesar* or *A Midsummer Night's Dream*.

During the work at school on the set play, you will have many opportunities to demonstrate your writing and reading skills. Many of these will involve the drafting and redrafting of your answers. You will also read the whole play and have a chance to develop a sense of the plot; establish for yourself the main characters and their characteristics; and work out how the chosen excerpt relates to the play as a whole. You may also discuss the main themes of the play and other aspects of it, like the dramatic tension and the language used. You may even have acted parts of it or seen a production.

The test offers you a different challenge. Now you will have to pace your writing so that you answer as well as you possibly can within the time limit. You are asked to complete one task in relation to one scene or part of a scene.

The best way to start your answer is to read the extract to remind yourself of its qualities and of its place in the play. You should then look again at the assignment and note the key words in it: what exactly is it asking you to look at and comment on? The next stage is to make notes, then to organise the main elements of your answer. You can make notes on the text, underlining or circling important passages and lines. Such preparation will help you write a better answer.

The pages which follow take you through several stages of assessing your performance. You are:

- reminded of the task;
- given pointers about what to include in your answer;
- provided with assessment criteria for gauging the quality of your work in relation to your 'understanding and response' and your 'written expression';
- shown sample answers by other students;
- supplied with detailed comments on those answers.

Paper 2 Answers

Task 1   Romeo and Juliet   Act 3 Scene 3, Lines 1–175

You will find the task on page 6.

REMINDER OF THE TASK
In this scene there is desperation and other extreme moods. There is also coolness and reason and even some admiration.

Show where these occur. Explain how they might affect the audience's feelings about Friar Lawrence at this point in the play.

Before you begin to write you should think about:

- Romeo's state of mind at the start of the scene;
- Romeo's state of mind at the end of the scene;
- What the Friar says to Romeo;
- What the Nurse says to the Friar.

Include some of these points in your answer:

- Romeo's desperation. Find examples in the scene of extreme language and extreme behaviour.
- the Friar's behaviour. Find examples. What do you think the audience thinks of the Friar?
- What are the Nurse's actions and words?
- Romeo is calmer at the end of the scene. Can you find evidence of this?
- the Nurse and Romeo expect the Friar to help. What do you think the audience want?

NOTE
A good way to answer this task is to take a narrative approach. That is, tell the story of what happens in this scene. But if this is all you do you will not be fully responding to the question and you will miss out on the high marks. You must also point out what and where the feelings and moods are because this is what the question asks. The question also wants to know what the audience might be feeling.

Paper 2 Answers

Task 2   Julius Caesar   Act 3 Scene 2, Lines 1–221

You will find the task on page 7.

REMINDER OF THE TASK
You are one of the Plebians listening and reacting to the speeches of Brutus and Mark Antony.

Explain what Brutus and Mark Antony have to say and its effect on you. Your mood will change during the scene. Explain why.

Before you begin to write you should think about:

- what happened before this scene and what happens after it;
- the ways in which your feelings change as you listen;
- the words Brutus uses to justify his actions;
- the ways in which Mark Antony sways the people listening with you;
- the different views of Brutus and Antony about Caesar's death.

Include some of these points in your answer:

- a comparison of the speeches of Brutus ('Romans, countrymen...') and Antony ('Friends, Romans, countrymen...'). Which is the more effective and why?
- an explanation of why Brutus' speech is in prose and Antony's in verse;
- the reaction of the Plebeians to the two speeches;
- a consideration of key words in the extract;
- the significance of this extract in the scene as a whole, and in the play as a whole.

NOTE
The secret to answering a question like this is to look at each part of the invitation to write in turn, and to structure your answer accordingly. So begin with an explanation of what Brutus and Antony have to say; then consider the effect on you (as a Plebeian and as yourself, in the audience – is there a difference?). Then register your changes of mood in the scene and link them to the significance of this scene in the play as a whole. Finally, make sure that you refer closely to the words of the scene to back up your observations.

Paper 2 Answers

Task 3 A Midsummer Night's Dream Act 4 Scene 1, Lines 43–211

You will find the task on page 8.

REMINDER OF THE TASK

This scene shows how the arguments and misunderstandings between the characters come to an end.

Think about Titania, Demetrius and Bottom. Does this scene make you believe that everything is sorted out for them?

Give reasons for what you think based on what the characters say and do in the scene.

Before you begin to write you should think about:

- the way Oberon and Titania settle their quarrel;
- what Demetrius says about his experiences;
- what Bottom says when he wakes up;
- the language the characters use to express their thoughts and feelings;
- whether you think that this scene ends happily for Titania, Demetrius and Bottom.

Include some of these points in your answer:

- what the language used by Bottom, Demetrius and Titania tells us about how they have or have not changed;
- Oberon has the changeling boy. This has changed his attitude towards Titania. He feels sorry (evidence?) for the cruel trick played on Titania. What trick?
- what is different about Demetrius?
- the connections between dreams and enchantment when compared to reality;
- dance and music show that Oberon and Titania are in harmony;
- the two couples discovered resting peacefully together is a sign that their quarrelling is over;
- you need to express your own opinion as to whether all the conflicts have been sorted out for good.

NOTE

You have been asked about Titania, Demetrius and Bottom. This does not mean that you can't mention any other characters but you have to mention the three you have been asked about more often.

Paper 2 Answers

How to assess and improve your response

The criteria that follow are to help you assess the quality of your own answers to the Shakespeare assignments, as well as to serve as general criteria when you come to look at the sample answers later in this book. As in Paper 1, these criteria will not only help you to assess your work; they will also help you to improve it by your noting what is expected at each of the levels.

25 marks are given for 'understanding and response to the text' based on the assessment criteria given below. Look back at your writing in the light of these criteria. Give yourself a mark, up to a maximum of 5 within each level, for each point included in your response. What level have you reached? If you get 6 marks or below, you are working at Level 3.

Fill in your marks on the chart on page 51.

READING ASSESSMENT CRITERIA: UNDERSTANDING OF AND RESPONSE TO THE TEXT

Marks 6–10

LEVEL 4
- Pupils select appropriate events.
- Some explanation is given to show their relevance to the task.

Marks 11–15

LEVEL 5
- Pupils give linked explanations that develop their views of what happens in the scene.
- Answers will be illustrated with some detail from the text.
- There may be limited reference to the effect on the audience.

Marks 16–20

LEVEL 6
- Pupils give a response which touches on all aspects of the task.
- Some of their commentaries are sustained.
- They explore the ways in which emotion is indicated or how reason and explanation are used.
- They show some insight in commenting on motives and feelings, the effects on the audience, or the language used in the scene.
- They use appropriate reference to the text to sustain these ideas.

Marks 21–25

LEVEL 7
- Pupils give a good, reasonably full answer, demonstrating a grasp of the task as a whole and commenting in detail on several aspects of it.
- They may be able to express a personal response to the feelings in the scene and examine ways in which an audience might be affected.
- They identify features of the language and show how these add to the mood of the scene.

Paper 2 Answers

How to assess and improve your written expression

As well as gauging the degree of understanding and response that each candidate achieves in reading Shakespeare, the end of key stage papers also test the accuracy and clarity of written expression in your answers.

15 marks are given for 'written expression' by the marker making a judgement about the quality of the writing as a whole. The number of correct or incorrect spellings are not counted as the mark awarded is based on overall achievement. So looking at the writing assessment criteria given below, a confident, easily understood, helpfully punctuated and paragraphed answer with most words spelt accurately would be given the full 15 marks. Look back at your writing in the light of these criteria. Award yourself a mark up to a maximum of 3 within each point included in your response. What level have you reached? A mark of 3 or less will place you at Level 3.

Fill in your marks on the chart on page 51.

WRITING ASSESSMENT CRITERIA: WRITTEN EXPRESSION INCLUDING HANDWRITING AND SPELLING

LEVEL 4 — *Marks 4–6*
- Ideas are arranged in an orderly way, making the meaning clear to the reader.
- Some complicated words are spelt correctly.
- Parts of the sentences are linked in a variety of ways, and the punctuation of them is mostly correct.
- Some use is made of paragraphs.
- Handwriting is clear and appears fluent.

LEVEL 5 — *Marks 7–9*
- The writing engages the interest of the reader.
- It is clearly structured by use of paragraphs.
- There is a variety of sentences appropriately punctuated and quite a wide range of complex words accurately spelt.
- Handwriting is readable and appears fluent.

LEVEL 6 — *Marks 10–12*
- The writing communicates well and ideas are grouped with a sense of purpose.
- It is clearly structured and language is used appropriately and interestingly, e.g. using a variety of sentence types.
- Paragraphs and punctuation are used well.
- Most of the words have been spelt correctly and the handwriting is consistently readable and fluent.

Paper 2 Answers

		Marks 13–15
L E V E L 7	• The writing is confident and the writer has made assured choices of words and style that are appropriate to the subject. • There is an understanding of the task and ideas have been clearly structured in answering it. • Paragraphing and punctuation are used correctly and spelling mistakes are errors caused by minor slips or the result of using specialised words. • Handwriting is consistently readable and appears fluent.	

These criteria are common to all three plays. When you have finished your work on understanding and response come back to this chart to gauge the quality of your written expression.

Paper 2
Sample answers

Task 1   Romeo and Juliet   Act 3 Scene 3, Lines 1–175

Use the specific assessment criteria below to gauge the quality of your answer to the *Romeo and Juliet* task. Then come back to them in your assessment of Nadia's answer.

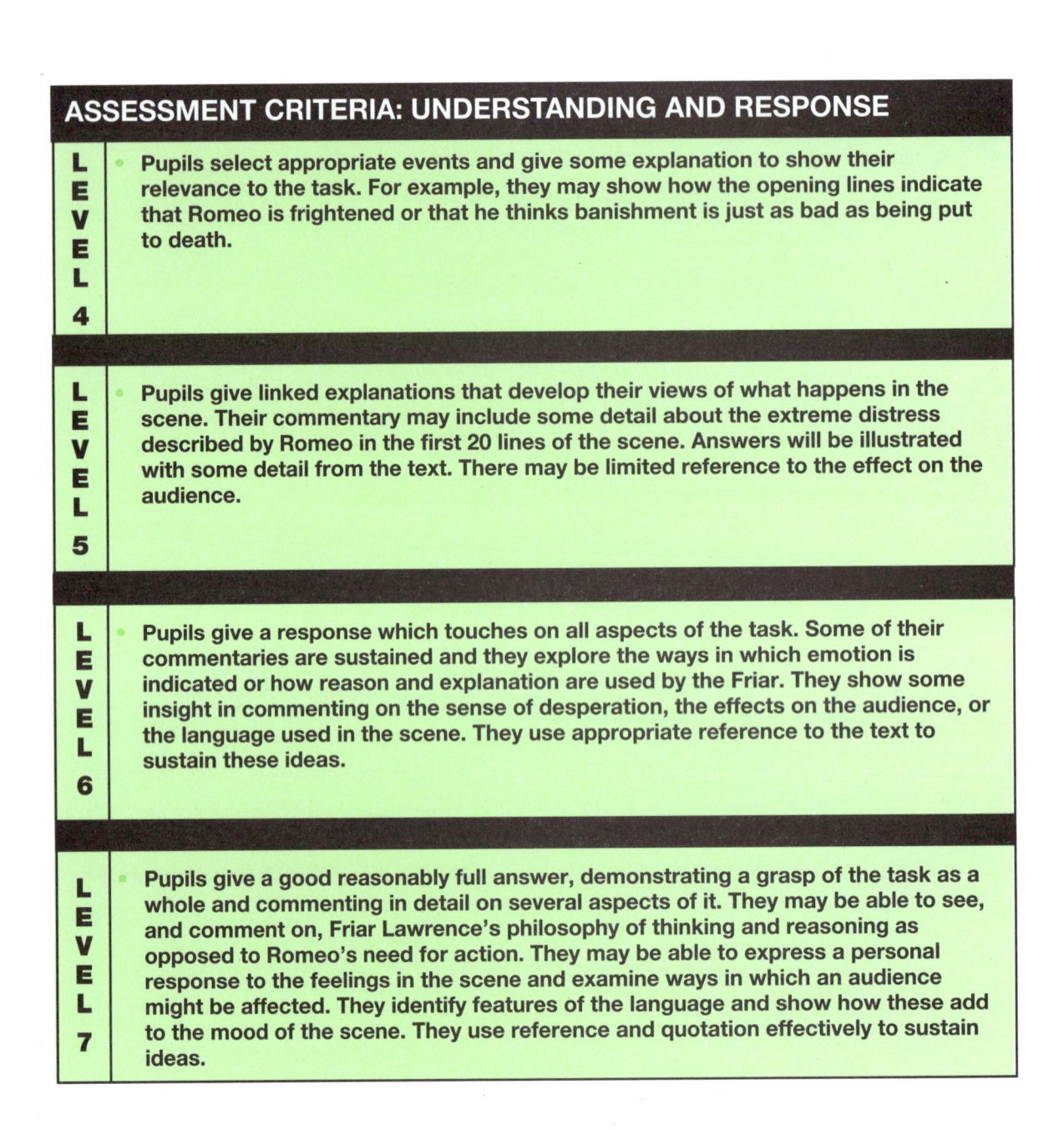

ASSESSMENT CRITERIA: UNDERSTANDING AND RESPONSE
LEVEL 4 • Pupils select appropriate events and give some explanation to show their relevance to the task. For example, they may show how the opening lines indicate that Romeo is frightened or that he thinks banishment is just as bad as being put to death.
LEVEL 5 • Pupils give linked explanations that develop their views of what happens in the scene. Their commentary may include some detail about the extreme distress described by Romeo in the first 20 lines of the scene. Answers will be illustrated with some detail from the text. There may be limited reference to the effect on the audience.
LEVEL 6 • Pupils give a response which touches on all aspects of the task. Some of their commentaries are sustained and they explore the ways in which emotion is indicated or how reason and explanation are used by the Friar. They show some insight in commenting on the sense of desperation, the effects on the audience, or the language used in the scene. They use appropriate reference to the text to sustain these ideas.
LEVEL 7 • Pupils give a good reasonably full answer, demonstrating a grasp of the task as a whole and commenting in detail on several aspects of it. They may be able to see, and comment on, Friar Lawrence's philosophy of thinking and reasoning as opposed to Romeo's need for action. They may be able to express a personal response to the feelings in the scene and examine ways in which an audience might be affected. They identify features of the language and show how these add to the mood of the scene. They use reference and quotation effectively to sustain ideas.

Paper 2
Sample answers

Nadia's answer

Consider this answer to Task 1, written by Nadia, a Year 9 student. Her errors have been corrected. Refer back to the specific criteria opposite and decide at what level you would place this answer.

You will find the task on page 6.

After fighting and killing Tybalt, Romeo rushed to Friar Lawrence in great fear to hide. He has not had time to think about the future. He does not know what is going to happen to him. He does not even know that he has been banished instead of being sentenced to death. When the Friar tells him, instead of being pleased, he says he would rather be dead, 'Be merciful, say "death".' Romeo says that he cannot live without seeing Juliet.

The Friar now reminds Romeo that he could have been executed. The audience might feel that the Friar is talking sense here and trying to calm Romeo down. But Romeo shouts 'Tis torture and not mercy.' The Friar says that Romeo is behaving like a madman and is still trying to get Romeo to listen to reason when there is loud knocking on the door. They are both frightened. It might be the Prince's men come to arrest Romeo but it is the Nurse.

She says Juliet is as upset and as mad with grief as Romeo.
'Blubbering and weeping, weeping and blubbering.'

The nurse doesn't know what to do. It is up to the Friar to sort it all out. The audience might feel that it is partly the Friar's fault anyway. The Nurse also expects the Friar to help.

When Romeo hears how wild with grief Juliet is he tries to stab himself. He is stopped by the Nurse and told off by the Friar. The audience will feel pleased that the two adults are keeping fairly cool. The Friar then clearly sets out for Romeo reasons why he should be happy. Tybalt tried to kill Romeo but Tybalt is the one dead; Juliet is alive; Romeo is banished, not executed; he might be forgiven by the Prince of Verona in the future and Romeo has got this night to spend with Juliet.

The Nurse admires the Friar for sorting this out,

'O Lord, I could have stayed here all the night
To hear good counsel'

The audience feel pleased that Romeo and Juliet will be together. Romeo is happy again.

Paper 2 Sample answers

During this scene the audience have observed feelings that have swung from fear and wild grief to admiration and happiness. At this stage in the play the audience might think that the Friar has sorted things out pretty well. In fact the Friar will never see Romeo alive again.

In my opinion the Friar as the adult who knew most of what was going on and who therefore had some control over who was told what, has to take at least some of the blame for the tragic outcome of this story.

Assessment of Nadia's answer

UNDERSTANDING AND RESPONSE TO THE TEXT

Nadia has answered this question in a narrative fashion without addressing the main focus of the assignment – the shift in moods in the scene – until the very end of her answer. She might think she is showing where the changes in mood occur, but her account is not explicit: it simply retells the story. Her opinion is given at the end, rather than a more considered analysis of how the mood changes might affect the audience's feelings about Friar Lawrence. In short, she hasn't really answered the question set. Suggested mark: 7, Level 4.

WRITTEN EXPRESSION

The writing is well set out and largely accurate: indeed, the quality of Nadia's written expression is higher than her demonstrated understanding of and response to the text. The following features are present:

- good use of paragraphs to structure the writing;
- quotations from the play written on separate lines and inside quotation marks;
- complex sentence structure;
- largely accurate spelling in her actual answers;
- the language style isn't entirely appropriate, as Nadia has written in simple narrative style rather than in a more analytical style that might use different ways of connecting sentences and paragraphs, e.g. 'on the one hand', 'despite', 'although' and 'nevertheless'.
- some of the language is loosely colloquial without being precise or illuminating, as in 'the Friar has sorted things out pretty well'.
- there is some repetition of phrases;
- some of the language is clichéd, as in 'wild with grief', without evidence from the text.

The overall quality of written expression, according to the criteria on pages 38–39, would seem to be about the bottom of Level 5: a mark of 8.

Paper 2
Sample answers

Task 2   Julius Caesar   Act 3 Scene 2

Use the specific assessment criteria below to gauge the quality of your answer to the *Julius Caesar* task. Then come back to them in your assessment of Lloyd's answer.

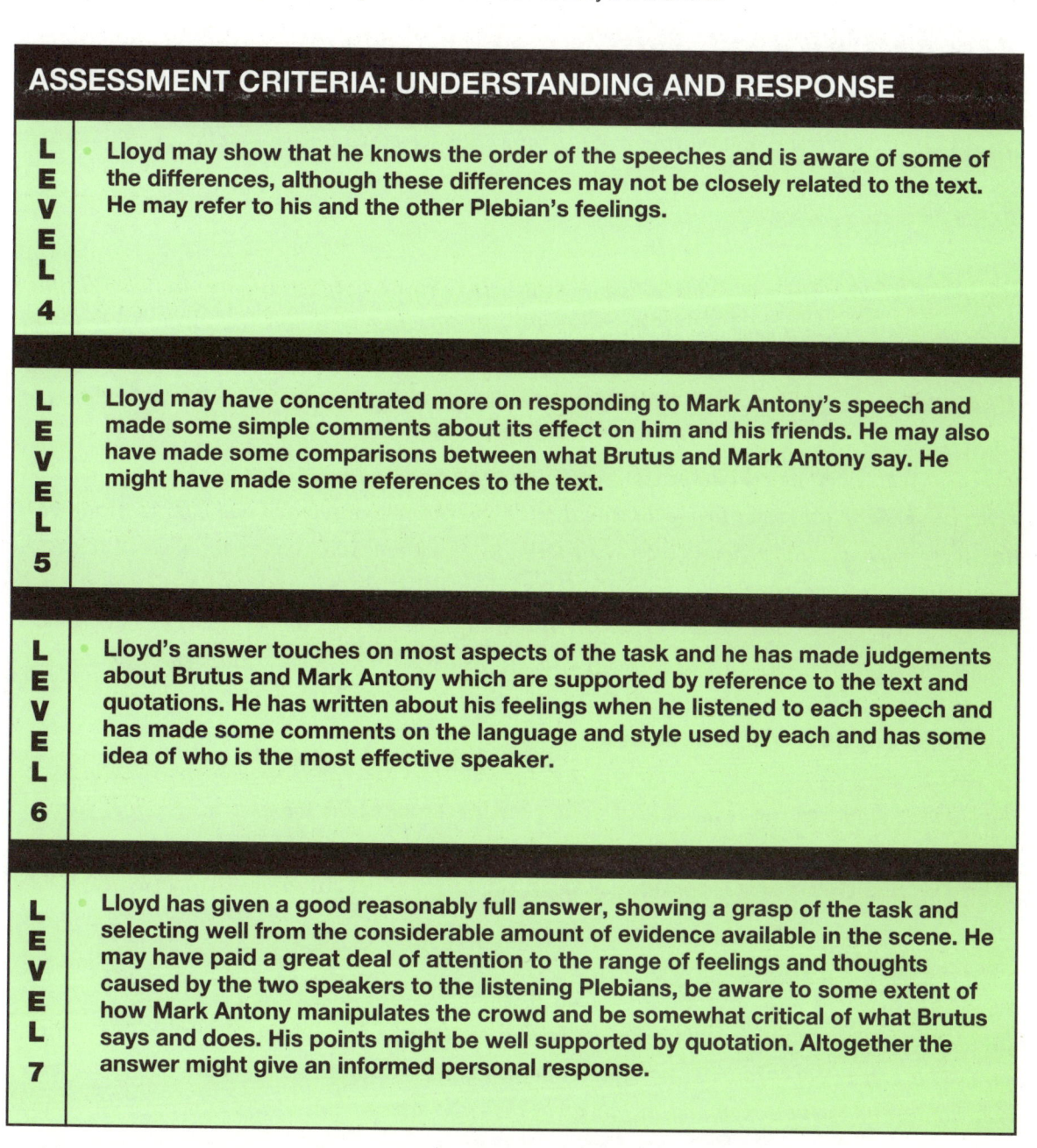

ASSESSMENT CRITERIA: UNDERSTANDING AND RESPONSE

LEVEL 4
- Lloyd may show that he knows the order of the speeches and is aware of some of the differences, although these differences may not be closely related to the text. He may refer to his and the other Plebian's feelings.

LEVEL 5
- Lloyd may have concentrated more on responding to Mark Antony's speech and made some simple comments about its effect on him and his friends. He may also have made some comparisons between what Brutus and Mark Antony say. He might have made some references to the text.

LEVEL 6
- Lloyd's answer touches on most aspects of the task and he has made judgements about Brutus and Mark Antony which are supported by reference to the text and quotations. He has written about his feelings when he listened to each speech and has made some comments on the language and style used by each and has some idea of who is the most effective speaker.

LEVEL 7
- Lloyd has given a good reasonably full answer, showing a grasp of the task and selecting well from the considerable amount of evidence available in the scene. He may have paid a great deal of attention to the range of feelings and thoughts caused by the two speakers to the listening Plebians, be aware to some extent of how Mark Antony manipulates the crowd and be somewhat critical of what Brutus says and does. His points might be well supported by quotation. Altogether the answer might give an informed personal response.

Paper 2 Sample answers

Lloyd's answer

Now consider this answer to Task 2, written by Lloyd, a Year 9 student. Most of his errors have been corrected. What level would you give it? Refer back to the specific criteria on page 43.

You will find the task on page 7.

Caesar, the leader of Rome has just been stabbed to death by some of his former supporters and friends. The plebians are swayed first one way and then the other. The final result is civil war.

Antony brings in Caesar.

We, the plebians, have just gathered here to hear what Brutus and Cassius have to say. We split into two groups to hear each side of the story. We already know what has happened to Caesar but we want to know why and we shall find out. I stayed in the group to hear Brutus and I'm glad I did. I, like so many others, loved Caesar, but after Brutus spoke, I didn't feel anything for the man.

Brutus explained all about Caesar. He gave us all the nonsense that he loved him and we all did believe him. Slowly I began to like Brutus. I felt I knew what he wanted and how to go about it and then he gave us the ultimate words. He loved us and loved Rome and wanted us all to live free from the end of Caesar and not all die slaves. That was it. We all wanted Brutus and wanted to forget what Caesar had for us. Of course Brutus explained all the other aspects of Caesar but we all felt we didn't need to hear them. It was all the usual things you would expect to hear.

'I loved him, he was ambitious, he loved you.'

But to us it didn't matter what he said, it all changed for me at the words he used which were,

'Had you rather Caesar were living, and die all slaves than that Caesar were dead, to live all free men?'

This, to me and also to other Plebians sent a message of what did he have in store for us and what would he have done with us, we didn't want to know, because now I felt I wanted Brutus to lead us, and I felt nothing would change this. But really this was not true, I felt kind of sorry for Caesar when Mark Antony carried him in over his shoulders, it was like did this man deserve it, what had he been through, was it fair what they had done to him. Brutus then left all alone telling us to listen to what Antony had to say. I really felt that Brutus, to should of stayed to mourn Caesar's body, but he didn't which was quite disappointing to us all Antony then spoke to us about Caesar, first saying what Brutus had said, but then to me he started to change what he was saying, he was putting doubts in what Brutus had said earlier by saying,

Paper 2 Sample answers

'But Brutus says he was ambitious
And Brutus is an honourable man...'

To me it was like he was saying that Brutus said he was ambitious but was Brutus ambitious as well and did he want us to feel the same way for him. Antony continued to speak about Brutus and Caesar and to me, his speech put across doubt of what Brutus had said earlier. When Antony finished in a dramatic way by saying,

'And I must pause till it come back to me.'

I suddenly felt all for Antony and Caesar. By this time my friends in the crowd were feeling the same, they began to doubt Brutus and what he had said and now we really did want to hear what else Mark Antony wanted to say.

When Antony started to talk again he explained his death was all wrong, that he deserved to live and that he loved us all, and then he suddenly shocked us all by telling us he had the Will of Caesar. Well really to all of us this was a great shock and now, really most of us had no doubt of what we felt for Caesar and Antony. We now know we wanted Caesar and all of us broke out into a shout of

'The Will, the Will! We will hear Caesar's Will.'

I really guess we were all curious of what Caesar was going to give us or Rome, so we all caused a great fuss to hear the Will, but at first Antony really refused to read it and said he was overcome by us for us wanting to hear it. I also believe he was afraid to read it, because of what Brutus and friends might do to him. Eventually, he saw sense and came down and talked to us about Caesar, he warned us about what he was going to say by

'If you have tears, prepare to shed them now.'

I think we all knew what this conversation was going to be about, his brutal death, and of course it was. He described in detail how the hole in his mantel was made and who made it. Each stab wound was described, bit by bit. It was so cruel what they did to Caesar and we all really felt sorry for the man. By this time we had forgotten about the Will, we were too taken aback by what Antony had said. We all wanted revenge and I believe most of us weren't going to give up with out. We really showed this with shouts of

'Revenge! About! Seek! Burn! Fire! Kill! Slay! Let not a traitor live!'

Paper 2
Sample answers

But in a way Antony calmed us down. He described he didn't want revenge and then for some reason reminded us all of the Will of Caesar. We all just suddenly remembered the Will and of course, as Antony promised, he read it to us. He left us money and his gardens and most of all his land on one side of the Tiber. We were overwhelmed by what had just been left and given to us, we now all loved Caesar and didn't want him dead, and we all went in search of revenge for Caesar's death.

Deep down I really felt for Caesar and then again I felt Mark Antony wanted us to feel that way for Caesar. Somehow I knew by the end of the speech we would want revenge, and soon after, revenge turned into Civil War which I believe was due to one speech said by Mark Antony.

Assessment of Lloyd's answer

UNDERSTANDING AND RESPONSE
Lloyd has written a full answer. He has a good idea of who is the most effective speaker and what devices were used to sway the crowd. He has made a very good attempt to imagine himself one of the Plebians which is what the task asked him to do. He also manages to suggest the range of feelings and thoughts caused by the two speakers. He supports some of his opinions by short quotations. His answer gains 23 marks, or a Level 7.

WRITTEN EXPRESSION
Reading Lloyd's answer you may notice how quickly he sets about answering the task set. His writing is confident and direct and his ideas clear. The following features are present:

- clearly indicated paragraphs;
- quotations from the play written on separate lines and set inside quotation marks;
- he is able to keep control of long sentences;
- he is able to put two or three simple sentences together into one more complicated sentence. For example, 'I, like so many others, loved Caesar, but after Brutus spoke, I didn't feel anything for the man.' This is a good 'writerly' style;
- sentences start with a capital letter and end with a full stop;
- in his actual answer his handwriting is easy to read.

There are just a few places where he is less confident. In the paragraph at the bottom of page 44, he misses out some question marks. He also writes 'should of stayed' instead of the Standard English 'should have stayed' and then later uses 'of' for 'about' in 'we were all curious of what Caesar was going to give us'.

Remember, this answer was written in an examination and the minor mistakes pointed out do not mean it is to be given a low score. You should consider the quality of the writing as a whole.

Although he sometimes spells 'Plebian' without a capital letter Lloyd's spelling is good. He only made one mistake. He wrote 'mantel' for 'mantle' which is the name for the loose, sleeveless cloak worn by Caesar.

Lloyd would gain 14 marks for his answer, or Level 7.

Paper 2 Sample answers

Task 3   A Midsummer Night's Dream   Act 4 Scene 1, Lines 43–211

Use the specific assessment criteria below to gauge the quality of your answer to the assignment for *A Midsummer Night's Dream*. Then come back to them in your assessment of Diane's answer.

ASSESSMENT CRITERIA: UNDERSTANDING AND RESPONSE

LEVEL 4
- There may be comments on Titania and Demetrius but not much about Bottom. There may be some simple comments about whether everything is better overall but generally thinking that for most of the characters it is. The answer might include some retelling of the scene.

LEVEL 5
- The answer gives some linked explanations that develop opinions about what happens to the characters. Some of the key points are covered and if the content of the scene is retold the writer has commented on some of the things that have happened. There may be a suggestion that Oberon and Titania will have trouble in the future. There may be some references to the words the characters use and how these show their state of bewilderment.

LEVEL 6
- All aspects of the task are touched on and the scene is referred to in some detail. The answer is focused on the task. Opinions are expressed on the extent to which the outcome is happy and the differences of the situations and reactions of the characters are indicated. For example, the answer might offer some detailed opinions about the behaviour of Oberon and Titania. There may be comments on the language of the characters, for example the difference between the words of Demetrius and Bottom. Appropriate evidence is used from the play to support opinions.

LEVEL 7
- This is a good, reasonably full answer, showing an understanding of the task. There may be comments in some detail on the extent to which everything is sorted out for each of the characters. The answer refers closely to the text when expressing opinions on Demetrius and Bottom's reactions when they wake. The language used by the characters is referred to and related to their thoughts and feelings. There may be a well developed personal response to one or more of the characters supported by well chosen, short quotations.

Paper 2
Sample answers

Diane's answer

Now consider this answer to Task 3, written by Diane, a Year 9 student. Her errors have been corrected. Refer back to the specific criteria on page 47 and decide at what level you would place this answer.

You will find the task on page 8.

Sleep and enchantment and dreams are part of this scene and of the play. Oberon's enchantment has caused Titania to fall in love with Bottom turned into an ass. When Oberon removes the enchantment and wakes her from her dream her feelings towards Oberon are gentle and not hostile:

'My Oberon, what visions have I seen!'

Oberon has somehow managed to acquire the changeling boy and so his feelings too are different. He now pities Titania and releases her from the enchantment. He calls her, 'my sweet Queen!'. Music plays and they dance together which is a sign that their quarrel is over. Although it might only be for as long as Titania does what Oberon wants.

Bottom's enchantment and changed appearance are also removed although when he does eventually wake up he will find no change in his general personality:

'Now when thou wakest, with thine own fool's eyes peep.'

He will find himself alone when he wakes up but able to remember enough of his vanished dream to want to write 'The Ballad of Bottom's dream'. That he is his old self is shown by the nonsense he talks:

'The eye of man has not heard, the ear of man has not seen, man's hand is not able to taste, his tongue to conceive, nor his heart to report what my dream was!'

For the time being, however, Bottom and the four lovers are sent even deeper into an enchanted sleep and this is how they are found by Theseus, Hippolyta and Egeus who are on an early morning hunting expedition. All the lovers are now in the same place and since this is Act 4 and towards the end of the play it is likely that things will be sorted out.

When Demetrius and the others are woken by the huntsmen it seems as if they are still enchanted because Demetrius says:

48

Paper 2
Sample answers

'Are you sure
That we are awake? It seems to me
That yet we sleep, we dream.'

He is amazed that his former love for Hermia has melted away. Unlike Bottom he seems to have been permanently changed by his enchantment and now for the first time returns Helena's love which will of course allow Hermia to marry Lysander whom she has always loved. Theseus approves and overrules Hermia's father who now accepts this state of affairs although at the start of the play he said that if Hermia didn't marry Demetrius she should be put to death.

The supposed enemies, Lysander and Demetrius, are peacefully found together. They both give what the audience know to be truthful answers to Theseus which indicates that trickery is over. I think that the main problems are sorted out, at least for the time being for Titania, Demetrius and Bottom. Although in the future Titania will have to be careful not to seriously cross Oberon, Demetrius may not be too reliable if ever the enchantment finally wears off and Bottom will continue to get himself into trouble.

Assessment of Diane's answer

UNDERSTANDING AND RESPONSE TO THE TEXT
This is a good answer from Diane. She has focussed on all three characters mentioned in the title of the assignment, though she does start slowly, meandering towards the main target of her piece: the resolution or otherwise for Titania, Demetrius and Bottom. One thing that does come out clearly in her answer is the different natures of the three characters, and she is sensitive to how the emergence from the dream is significant to each of them.

Although she refers well to the text, she does not develop her insightful ideas very far; instead, she rather hastily comes to conclusions without considering the details of the language. She seems to see the characters in the play as 'real' rather than as creations by Shakespeare, although she is aware of the difference between how the characters see events and how the audience sees them.

The quality of the understanding as evidenced in the response seems to suggest a mark of 17 or 18 at Level 6. What do you think?

WRITTEN EXPRESSION
Diane writes well. Her expression is clear, communicative and largely accurate. She exhibits the following strengths in her writing:

- use of complex sentence structure, as in 'That he is his old self is shown by...';
- accurate spelling in her actual answer;
- good use of paragraphs to indicate the structure of her thinking and expression;
- reference to the assignment's title: she methodically thinks about each of the characters in turn;

Paper 2
Sample answers

- good use of quotations to support her argument, as well as elegant presentation of these quotations on separate lines and in quotation marks;
- comparison between the characters, evidenced in her use of connecting words, as in 'Unlike Bottom...'.

Perhaps the main weakness is that the short paragraphs do not allow for much development of her thoughts, as suggested in the 'Understanding and Response' section above.

Suggested mark for written expression: 13 at Level 6.

Finding your level for English

Make a note of your marks on this chart:

	Paper 1				Paper 2		
	1	2	3	4	Task		
Possible marks	15	15	20	30	25 + 15	Possible score: 120
Your marks					+	Your score:

Converting your marks into a level

Your score	Level
35–64	4
65–94	5
95–124	6
125–150	7

Talking in whispers

This is part of a novel by James Watson. It is set in Chile, during the 1970s. The country is ruled by a right-wing military dictatorship. Political prisoners are being taken by the army to the National Stadium. Andres, a teenage boy, is searching for his friend, Braulio.

Andres stayed clear of the crowd. He watched the arrival of another truck. The soldiers did not care if their brutality was witnessed by hundreds of people. Those prisoners who hesitated as they climbed from the truck were hastened on their way with rifle butts.

'Move, scum!'

Suddenly Andres broke forward, seeking a gap in the wall of people. 'Braulio!' There was no doubt. His friend had jumped from the truck. He was handcuffed. 'Braulio!' Andres fought to get through the crowd.

Braulio Altuna stood a head taller than the other prisoners in line. A stream of blood had congealed down one side of his face.

Andres forgot his own danger. He must go to Braulio, at the very least let him know that somebody had proof that he was alive.

Please – please let me through – my friend is out there! Andres looked to be having no luck in prising a way through the crowd when he spotted a tall man in a white mack, making better progress.

'Permiso! Give us a passage, folks – it's for a good cause.'

An American.

Andres tucked himself in behind the man, burly, fair-haired, with out-thrust arm, shoving a sideways path towards the truck and the gates of the stadium.

Andres got so close to the American that he could have picked his pocket. He glanced down and saw that the man was holding something behind him, wrapped in a carrier bag.

For an instant, Andres decided that the American had a gun. Yet the compulsion to make contact with Braulio proved greater that Andres' fear that he might have landed himself in a shoot-out.

The object which the American slipped from the carrier bag had indeed many more shots than a pistol. A camera! He's a pressman. Andres felt a thrill of hope. Here comes the American cavalry! He was right behind the pressman. He shouted in Spanish:

'Give him room!' And then in a low voice only audible to the American, 'The world's got to know what's happening here.'

'You bet it has.' The pressman took Andres in in one friendly – even grateful – glance. They were comrades. Together they breasted a way through the crowd.

'That my friend – the tall one.'

The last prisoners were being driven from the truck. One was not fast enough to please his guards. He was hurt, hobbling, gripping his side in pain.

'Step on it, you red scab!'

The American's camera was in the air. A rifle butt swung against the stumbling prisoner.

Click-whirr, click-whirr – the scene was banked, recorded.

Braulio had turned, stepping out of line. He protested at the guard's action and immediately drew soldiers round him like wasps to honey.

Click-whirr, click-whirr. The toppling of Braulio was captured. Here was evidence for the time when villainy would be brought to justice.

Yet here also was terrible danger. The American photographer had himself been snapped by the eye of the officer commanding the troops. 'Christ. They've spotted me!' He lowered his camera swiftly below the shoulders of the crowd. He shifted, half-face towards Andres. He seemed paralysed by fear.

The American pushed the camera into Andres' hand. 'Take this – I'm finished.'

'But –'

'I beg you. The film in that camera...'

The officer and his men were clubbing a passage through the crowd towards the American. Andres ducked the camera through the open zip of his jacket 'Who shall I say!' He was being carried away from the pressman by the retreat of the crowds.

'Chailey – Don Chailey!' He yelled the name of his newspaper too but the words did not carry to Andres who found himself squeezed step by step away from the oncoming troops.

The crowd had saved Andres. It had no power to delay sentence upon the American. The soldiers were all round him. Momentarily his fair hair could be seen between their helmets. Then his arms went up above his head. He folded under a rampage of blows. He was hammered to the ground. He was kicked in the body, in the head, his hands stamped upon, his ribs skewered with iron-shod boots.

And now they were searching for his camera. They were demanding answers from the crowd, accusing them, turning their violence upon the innocent, frisking everyone who could have been within orbit of the American.

For an eternal second, Andres stood and watched. He saw Don Chailey dragged towards the stadium entrance. He saw him flung into one of the turnstiles.

Andres trembled as if touched by an electrified fence. Till now, he had wandered helplessly, insignificant. Soaked to the skin, he had arrived at the final blank wall and closed gate. His brain, his heart, his passionate resolve – they were nothing in the face of the Junta's untouchable strength.

But now... A chance in a million, an encounter lasting no longer than two minutes, had changed everything. He was in possession of something the military would like to get their hands on – proof of their brutality. What's more, Andres was witness to what the Black Berets had done to a citizen of the United States of America.

The Americans don't pour millions of dollars into Chile for us to beat up their newspapermen. Andres was at the street corner, poised for flight. All at once he had a purpose, a direction, a next step. He tapped the camera reverently. Somehow I must contact the Resistance. What's in this camera might be just as valuable as bullets.

"They won't kill me now they know that someone knows about me..."

AMNESTY INTERNATIONAL – 30 YEARS FIGHTING FOR THE VICTIMS OF INJUSTICE

Amnesty International was founded in 1961 by Peter Benenson, a British lawyer. It started by campaigning for "prisoners of conscience", people who were behind bars simply because of who they were or what they believed, and confronted related issues such as unfair trials, torture and executions.

Since 1961 Amnesty International has campaigned on behalf of 43,500 individuals. Of these cases, 40,500 have now been closed.

Street arrest in Madagascar.

PRINTED ON ENVIRONMENTALLY FRIENDLY PAPER

The organisation spans all political, religious, ethnic and age groups. But members are united by a common belief: that by coming together we can all help stop human rights abuses, wherever they occur. Amnesty International does not seek nor receive any money from any government, but relies solely on donations from the public.

**Amnesty International,
99-119 Rosebery Avenue, London EC1R 4RE.**

The words printed on the front of this brochure are taken from a letter from a former Prisoner of Conscience and tell in their own way how effective Amnesty International can be in bringing hope to victims of brutal injustice. The letter continues:

"*....because before that we didn't have a real hope to leave prison alive. They sent thousands of letters to me in prison - [the guards] never gave them to me, but they were aware somewhere in the world thousands of people knew about me*"

12 year old Manoj Singh, India.

HELP FIGHT FOR VICTIMS OF BRUTAL INJUSTICE.

By joining Amnesty International you can help make a real difference to the lives of ordinary people who face the vilest abuses such as imprisonment, torture, rape and death, simply for expressing their peacefully held beliefs, being the wrong colour or belonging to the wrong ethnic group or religion.

People like Jairam Singh who went to a Delhi police station with his 12-year old son Manoj, who was arrested on suspicion of stealing a purse. Without ever registering a case against him, they tortured Jairam Singh to death.

Daily we receive reports of such sickening abuse carried out in countries throughout the world. Scores of governments let their police and soldiers get away with beating, inflicting electric shocks or raping prisoners to humiliate or force them to sign false confessions.

```
"If there's a lot of pressure, like
from Amnesty International, we might
pass the political prisoners on to a
judge. But if there's no pressure,
then they're dead."
```
Former torturer in El Salvador

Please show your commitment to human rights by joining Amnesty International today.

SOME CURRENT CASES THAT GIVE AMNESTY INTERNATIONAL CAUSE FOR CONCERN

"PRISONERS OF CONSCIENCE"

In South Korea Kim Song Man was sentenced to death as a North Korean spy. This has now been commuted to life imprisonment. Apart from his confession - which he claims was extracted by torture - no evidence was ever produced that he had been a spy.

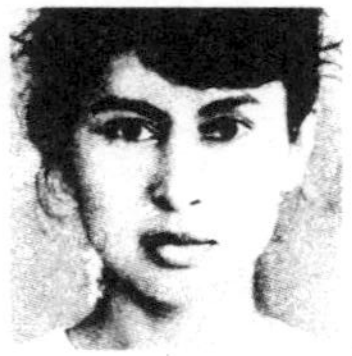

Aung San Suu Kyi lives in Myanmar (formerly Burma), where she is General Secretary of the National League for Democracy. However, despite her party's election victory in 1990 she remains under house arrest.

"DISAPPEARED"

Jose Ramon Garcia Gomez left home for a political meeting in December 1988 in Mexico. He never arrived and has since "disappeared". Enquiries held into his whereabouts have proved that he was abducted by members of the security forces.

On the morning of 29 April 1992 Harjit Singh was arrested at a bus-stop in India by a group of police officers. He has since "disappeared", with police denying all knowledge of the arrest.

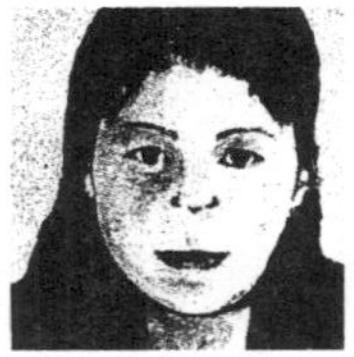

Having been detained by the army in Peru, 15 year-old Elisa Allca Lima has now "disappeared", with military authorities refusing to acknowledge her detention.

HOW AMNESTY INTERNATIONAL'S WORK SAVES LIVES

Amnesty International works by highlighting brutal injustices wherever they occur around the world. Amnesty publishes the facts on torture and unfair imprisonment ... asks questions of governments which appear guilty of human rights abuse ... campaigns against execution and brings hope to thousands of victims through concerted letter writing campaigns that embarrass guilty governments and often mean life rather than death for the prisoner.

Victims of chemical weapons, IRAQ.

Amnesty International believes that if people around the world force governments to take up these challenges, human rights can be defended honestly, vigorously and successfully.

WHAT CAN YOU DO TO HELP?

Become a member of Amnesty International. All you have to do is return the membership form today, together with your subscription fee. By doing so you will have added your voice to a special group of people in over 150 countries who are prepared to speak out on behalf of human rights around the world.

LETTERS FROM PRISONERS AND THEIR FAMILIES

We receive many letters from former prisoners and their families that lay testament to the success of our campaigns. For each prisoner on whose behalf we work, there are many more who have disappeared or are held in secret detention.

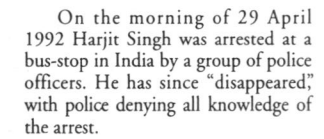

"My mother and I - in fact the whole family - cannot find words appropriate and strong enough to express our gratitude for both the moral and material support given to the family during my two years and four months stay in detention without trial."

Former South African Prisoner of Conscience

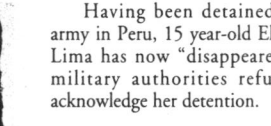

```
"At last, I can enjoy the immense
pleasure of writing to you as a free
man. Yes! I'm a free man and I feel
so much pleasure and excitement about
being able to kiss and hug my wife,
my children, my parents, brothers,
sisters, family, and friends, not to
mention the strangers who have
welcomed me with open arms."
```

Former Kenyan Prisoner of Conscience

"Without your support, concern and love, I would not have survived the prison brutality and barbarity."

Former Argentine Prisoner of Conscience

"Well, the impossible and the totally unexpected has happened and I am still stunned! ... I would like to say thank you for all you have done for us. Your sympathy, kindness and selfless efforts to help us during the terrible nightmare is something the children and I can never, never forget, nor be able to adequately thank you."

Former Pakistan Prisoner of Conscience

Romeo and Juliet
Act 3 Scene 3, Lines 1–175
Friar Lawrence's cell

Enter FRIAR LAWRENCE.

FRIAR LAWRENCE   Romeo, come forth, come forth, thou fearful man:
Affliction is enamoured of thy parts,
And thou art wedded to calamity.

Enter ROMEO.

ROMEO   Father, what news? What is the Prince's doom?
What sorrow craves acquaintance at my hand,   5
That I yet know not?

FRIAR LAWRENCE   Too familiar.
Is my dear son with such sour company!
bring thee tidings of the Prince's doom.

ROMEO   What less than doomsday is the Prince's doom?

FRIAR LAWRENCE   A gentler judgement vanished from his lips: 10
Not body's death, but body's banishment.

ROMEO   Ha, banishment? be merciful, say 'death':
For exile hath more terror in his look,
Much more than death. Do not say 'banishment'!

FRIAR LAWRENCE   Here from Verona art thou banishèd.   15
Be patient, for the world is broad and wide.

ROMEO   There is no world without Verona walls,
But purgatory, torture, hell itself:
Hence 'banishèd' is banished from the world,
And world's exile is death; then 'banishèd'   20
Is death mistermed. Calling death 'banishèd',
Thou cut'st my head off with a golden axe,
And smilest upon the stroke that murders me.

FRIAR LAWRENCE   O deadly sin! O rude unthankfulness!
Thy fault our law calls death, but the kind Prince,   25
Taking thy part, hath rushed aside the law,
And turned that black word 'death', to 'banishment'.
This is dear mercy, and thou seest it not.

ROMEO   'Tis torture, and not mercy. Heaven is here
Where Juliet lives, and every cat and dog   30
And little mouse, every unworthy thing,
Live here in heaven, and may look on her,
But Romeo may not. More validity,
More honourable state, more courtship lives
In carrion flies than Romeo; they may seize   35
On the white wonder of dear Juliet's hand,
And steal immortal blessing from her lips,
Who even in pure and vestal modesty
Still blush, as thinking their own kisses sin;
But Romeo may not, he is banishèd.   40
Flies may do this, but I from this must fly;
They are free men, but I am banishèd:
And sayest thou yet that exile is not death?
Hadst thou no poison mixed, no sharp-ground knife,
No sudden mean of death, though ne'er so mean,   45
But 'banishèd' to kill me? 'banishèd'?
O Friar, the damnèd use that word in hell;
Howling attends it. How hast thou the heart,
Being a divine, a ghostly confessor,
A sin-absolver, and my friend professed,   50
To mangle me with that word 'banishèd'?

FRIAR LAWRENCE   Thou fond mad man, hear me a little speak.

ROMEO   O thou wilt speak again of banishment.

FRIAR LAWRENCE   I'll give thee armour to keep off that word:
Adversity's sweet milk, philosophy,   55

	To comfort thee though thou art banishèd.	
ROMEO	Yet 'banishèd'? Hang up philosophy! Unless philosophy can make a Juliet, Displant a town, reserve a prince's doom, It helps not, it prevails not; talk no more.	60
FRIAR LAWRENCE	O then I see that mad men have no ears.	
ROMEO	How should they when that wise men have no eyes?	
FRIAR LAWRENCE	Let me dispute with thee of thy estate.	
ROMEO	Thou canst not speak of that thou dost not feel. Wert thou as young as I, Juliet thy love, An hour but married, Tybalt murderèd, Doting like me, and like me banishèd, Then mightst thou speak, then mightst thou tear thy hair, And fall upon the ground as I do now, Taking the measure of an unmade grave.	65 70

Enter NURSE *[within] and knock.*

FRIAR LAWRENCE	Arise, one knocks, Good Romeo, hide thyself.	
ROMEO	Not I, unless the breath of heart-sick groans Mist-like infold me from the search of eyes.	

Knock.

FRIAR LAWRENCE	Hark how they knock! Who's there? – Romeo, arise, Thou wilt be taken. – Stay a while! – Stand up;	75

Loud knock.

Run to my study. – By and by! – God's will,
What simpleness is this? – I come, I come!

Knock.

Who knocks so hard? whence come you? what's your will?

NURSE	*[Within]* Let me come in, and you shall know my errand: I come from Lady Juliet.	
FRIAR LAWRENCE	Welcome then. *[Unlocks the door.]*	80

Enter NURSE.

NURSE	O holy Friar, O tell me, holy Friar, Where's my lady's lord? where's Romeo?	
FRIAR LAWRENCE	There on the ground, with his own tears made drunk.	
NURSE	O he is even in my mistress' case, Just in her case. O woeful sympathy! Piteous predicament! even so lies she, Blubb'ring and weeping, weeping and blubb'ring. Stand up, stand up, stand and you be a man; For Juliet's sake, for her sake, rise and stand; Why should you fall into so deep an O?	85 90
ROMEO	Nurse! *[He rises].*	
NURSE	Ah, sir, ah, sir, death's the end of all.	
ROMEO	Spakest thou of Juliet? how is it with her? Doth not she think me an old murderer, Now I have stained the childhood of our joy With blood removed but little from her own? Where is she? and how doth she? and what says My concealed lady to our cancelled love?	95
NURSE	O she says nothing, sir, but weeps and weeps, And now falls on her bed, and then starts up, And Tybalt calls, and then on Romeo cries, And then down falls again,	100
ROMEO	As if that name, Shot from the deadly level of a gun,	

		Did murder her, as that name's cursèd hand		
		Murdered her kinsman. O tell me, Friar, tell me,	105
		In what vile part of this anatomy		
		Doth my name lodge? Tell me, that I may sack		
		The hateful mansion.		

He offers to stab himself, and NURSE *snatches the dagger away.*

FRIAR LAWRENCE	Hold thy desperate hand!	
	Art thou a man? thy form cries out thou art;	
	Thy tears are womanish, thy wild acts denote	110
	The unreasonable fury of a beast.	
	Unseemly woman in a seeming man,	
	And ill-beseeming beast in seeming both,	
	Thou hast amazed me. By my holy order,	
	I thought thy disposition better tempered.	115
	Hast thou slain Tybalt? wilt thou slay thyself,	
	And slay thy lady that in thy life lives,	
	By doing damnèd hate upon thyself?	
	Why rail'st thou on thy birth? the heaven and earth?	
	Since birth, and heaven, and earth, all three do meet	120
	In thee at once, which thou at once wouldst lose.	
	Fie, fie, thou sham'st thy shape, thy love, thy wit,	
	Which like a usurer abound'st in all,	
	And usest none in that true use indeed	
	Which should bedeck thy shape, thy love, thy wit:	125
	Thy noble shape is but a form of wax,	
	Digressing from the valour of a man;	
	Thy dear love sworn but hollow perjury,	
	Killing that love which thou hast vowed to cherish;	
	Thy wit, that ornament to shape and love,	130
	Misshapen in the conduct of them both,	
	Like powder in a skilless soldier's flask,	
	Is set afire by thine own ignorance,	
	And thou dismembered with thine own defence.	
	What, rouse thee, man! thy Juliet is alive,	135
	For whose dear sake thou wast but lately dead:	
	There art thou happy. Tybalt would kill thee,	
	But thou slewest Tybalt: there art thou happy.	
	The law that threatened death becomes thy friend,	
	And turns it to exile: there art thou happy.	140
	A pack of blessings light upon thy back,	
	Happiness courts thee in her best array,	
	But like a mishavèd and sullen wench,	
	Thou pouts upon thy fortune and thy love:	
	Take heed, take heed, for such die miserable.	145
	Go get thee to thy love as was decreed,	
	Ascend her chamber, hence and comfort her;	
	But look thou stay not till the Watch be set,	
	For then thou canst not pass to Mantua,	
	Where thou shalt live till we can find a time	150
	To blaze your marriage, reconcile your friends,	
	Beg pardon of the Prince, and call thee back	
	With twenty hundred thousand times more joy	
	Than thou went'st forth in lamentation.	
	Go before, Nurse, commend me to thy lady,	155
	And bid her hasten all the house to bed,	
	Which heavy sorrow makes them apt unto.	
	Romeo is coming.	
NURSE	O Lord, I could have stayed here all the night	
	To hear good counsel. O, what learning is!	160
	My lord, I'll tell my lady you will come.	
ROMEO	Do so, and bid my sweet prepare to chide.	

NURSE offers to go in, and turns again.

NURSE	Here, sir, a ring she bid me give you, sir.	
	Hie you, make haste, for it grows very late.	
ROMEO	How well my comfort is revived by this.	165

Exit NURSE.

FRIAR LAWRENCE   Go hence, good night, and here stands all your state:
Either be gone before the Watch be set,
Or by the break of day disguised from hence.
Sojourn in Mantua; I'll find out your man,
And he shall signify from time to time   170
Every good hap to you that chances here.
Give me thy hand, 'tis late. Farewell, good night.

ROMEO   But that a joy past joy calls out on me,
It were a grief, so brief to part with thee:
Farewell.   175

Exeunt.

Julius Caesar
Act 3 Scene 2, Lines 1–21
Rome   The market-place

Enter BRUTUS *and* CASSIUS *with the* PLEBEIANS.

ALL   We will be satisfied! Let us be satisfied!

BRUTUS   Then follow me and give me audience, friends.
Cassius, go you into the other street
And part the numbers.
Those that will hear me speak, let 'em stay here;   5
Those that will follow Cassius, go with him;
And public reasons shall be renderèd
Of Caesar's death.

1 PLEBEIAN   I will hear Brutus speak.

2 PLEBEIAN   I will hear Cassius and compare their reasons
When severally we hear them renderèd.   10

Exit CASSIUS *with some of the* PLEBEIANS.

BRUTUS *goes into the pulpit.*

3 PLEBEIAN   The noble Brutus is ascended, silence!

BRUTUS   Be patient till the last.
Romans, countrymen, and lovers, hear me for my cause, and be silent
that you may hear. Believe me for mine honour, and have respect to
mine honour that you may believe. Censure me in your wisdom, and   15
awake your senses that you may the better judge. If there be any
in this assembly, any dear friend of Caesar's, to him I say that Brutus'
love to Caesar was no less than his. If then that friend demand why
Brutus rose against Caesar, this is my answer: not that I loved Caesar
less, but that I loved Rome more. Had you rather Caesar were living,   20
and die all slaves, than that Caesar were dead, to love all freeman? As
Caesar loved me, I weep for him; as he was fortunate, I rejoice at it; as
he was valiant, I honour him; but, as he was ambitious, I slew him.
There is tears for his love, joy for his fortune, honour for his valour,
and death for his ambition. Who is here so base that would be a   25
bondman? If any, speak, for him have I offended. Who is here so rude
that would not be a Roman? If any, speak, for him I have offended.
Who is here so vile that will not love his country? If any, speak, for
him I offended. I pause for a reply.

ALL   None, Brutus, none.   30

BRUTUS   Then none have I offended. I have done no more to Caesar than you
shall do to Brutus. The question of his death is enrolled in the
Capital, his glory not extenuated wherein he was worthy, nor his
offences enforced for which he suffered death.

Enter MARK ANTONY *[and others] with Caesar's body.*

Here comes his body, mourned by Mark Antony, who, though he had   35
no hand in his death, shall receive the benefit of his dying, a place in
the commonwealth, as which of you shall not? With this I depart: that,
as I slew my best lover for the good of Rome, I have the same dagger
for myself when it shall please my country to need my death.

Comes down.

ALL   Live Brutus, live, live!   40

1 PLEBEIAN   Bring him with triumph home unto his house.

2 PLEBEIAN   Give him a statue with his ancestors.

3 PLEBEIAN   Let him be Caesar.

4 PLEBEIAN   Caesar's better parts
Shall be crowned in Brutus.

1 PLEBEIAN   We'll bring him to his house
With shouts and clamours.

BRUTUS   My countrymen –   45

2 PLEBEIAN	Peace, silence, Brutus speaks!	
1 PLEBEIAN	Peace ho!	
BRUTUS	Good countrymen, let me depart alone,	
	And, for my sake, stay here with Antony.	
	Do grace to Caesar's corpse, and grace his speech	
	Tending to Caesar's glories, which Mark Antony	50
	(By our permission) is allowed to make.	
	I do entreat you, not a man depart,	
	Save I alone, till Antony have spoke. [*Exit.*]	
1 PLEBEIAN	Stay ho, and let us hear Mark Antony.	
3 PLEBEIAN	Let him go up into the public chair,	55
	We'll hear him. Noble Antony, go up.	
ANTONY	For Brutus' sake, I am beholding to you.	
	Goes into the pulpit.	
4 PLEBEIAN	What does he say of Brutus?	
3 PLEBEIAN	He says for Brutus' sake	
	He finds himself beholding to us all.	
4 PLEBEIAN	'Twere best he speak no harm of Brutus here!	60
1 PLEBEIAN	This Caesar was a tyrant.	
3 PLEBEIAN	Nay, that's certain:	
	We are blest that Rome is rid of him.	
2 PLEBEIAN	Peace, let us hear what Antony can say.	
ANTONY	You gentle Romans –	
ALL	Peace ho, let us hear him.	
ANTONY	Friends, Romans, countrymen, lend me your ears!	65
	I come to bury Caesar, not to praise him.	
	The evil that men do lives after them,	
	The good is oft interrèd with their bones:	
	So let it be with Caesar. The noble Brutus	
	Hath told you Caesar was ambitious;	70
	If it were so, it was a grievous fault,	
	And grievously hath Caesar answered it.	
	Here, under leave of Brutus and the rest –	
	For Brutus is an honourable man,	
	So are they all, all honourable men –	75
	Come I to speak in Caesar's funeral.	
	He was my friend, faithful and just to me,	
	But Brutus says he was ambitious,	
	And Brutus is an honourable man.	
	He hath brought many captives home to Rome,	80
	Whose ransoms did the general coffers fill;	
	Did this in Caesar seem ambitious?	
	When that the poor have cried, Caesar hath wept:	
	Ambition should be made of sterner stuff;	
	Yet Brutus says he was ambitious,	85
	And Brutus is an honourable man.	
	You all did see that on the Lupercal	
	I thrice presented him a kingly crown,	
	Which he did thrice refuse. Was this ambition?	
	Yet Brutus says he was ambitious,	90
	And sure he is an honourable man.	
	I speak not to disprove what Brutus spoke,	
	But here I am to speak what I do know.	
	You all did love him once, not without cause;	
	What cause withholds you then to mourn for him?	95
	O judgement, thou art fled to brutish beasts,	
	And men have lost their reason! Bear with me,	
	My heart is in the coffin there with Caesar,	
	And I must pause till it come back to me.	
1 PLEBEIAN	Methinks there is much reason in his sayings,	100
2 PLEBEIAN	If thou consider rightly of the matter,	

	Caesar has had great wrong.	
3 PLEBEIAN	Has he, masters! I fear there will a worse come in his place.	
4 PLEBEIAN	Marked ye his words? He would not take the crown, Therefore 'tis certain he was not ambitious.	105
1 PLEBEIAN	If it be found so, some will dear abide it.	
2 PLEBEIAN	Poor soul, his eyes are red as fire with weeping.	
3 PLEBEIAN	There's not a nobler man in Rome than Antony.	
4 PLEBEIAN	Now mark him, he begins again to speak.	
ANTONY	But yesterday the word of Caesar might Have stood against the world; now lies he there, And none so poor to do him reverence. O masters, if I were disposed to stir Your hearts and minds to mutiny and rage, I should do Brutus wrong and Cassius wrong, Who (you all know) are honourable men. I will not do them wrong; I rather choose To wrong the dead, to wrong myself and you, Than I will wrong such honourable men. But here's a parchment with the seal of Caesar, I found it in his closet, 'tis his will. Let but the commons hear his testament – Which, pardon me, I do not mean to read – And they would go and kiss dead Caesar's wounds And dip their napkins in his sacred blood, Yea, beg a hair of him for memory, And, dying, mention it within their wills, Bequeathing it as a rich legacy Unto their issue.	110 115 120 125
4 PLEBEIAN	We'll hear the will. Read it, Mark Antony.	130
ALL	The will, the will, we will hear Caesar's will!	
ANTONY	Have patience, gentle friends, I must not read it. It is not meet you know how Caesar loved you: You are not wood, you are not stones, but men, And, being men, hearing the will of Caesar, It will inflame you, it will make you mad. 'Tis good you know not that you are his heirs, For if you should, O, what would come of it?	 135
4 PLEBEIAN	Read the will, we'll hear it, Antony. You shall read us the will, Caesar's will!	140
ANTONY	Will you be patient? Will you stay awhile? I have o'ershot myself to tell you of it. I fear I wrong the honourable men Whose daggers have stabbed Caesar, I do fear it.	
4 PLEBEIAN	They were traitors. Honourable men!	145
ALL	The will! The testament!	
2 PLEBEIAN	They were villians, murderers! The will, read the will!	
ANTONY	You will compel me then to read the will? Then make a ring about the corpse of Caesar And let me show you him that made the will. Shall I descend? And will you give me leave?	 150
ALL	Come down.	
2 PLEBEIAN	Descend.	
3 PLEBEIAN	You shall have leave.	

ANTONY comes down from the pulpit.

4 PLEBEIAN	A ring, stand round.	155
1 PLEBEIAN	Stand from the hearse, stand from the body.	
2 PLEBEIAN	Room for Antony, most noble Antony.	

ANTONY	Nay, press not so upon me, stand far off.	
ALL	Stand back! Room, bear back!	
ANTONY	If you have tears, prepare to shed them now.	160
	You all do know this mantle. I remember	
	The first time ever Caesar put it on,	
	'Twas on a summer's evening, in his tent,	
	That day he overcame the Nervii.	
	Look, in this place ran Cassius' dagger through;	165
	See what a rent the envious Casca made;	
	Through this the well-belovèd Brutus stabbed,	
	And as he plucked his cursèd steel away,	
	Mark how the blood of Caesar followed it,	
	As rushing out of doors to be resolved	170
	If Brutus so unkindly knocked or no,	
	For Brutus, as you know, was Caesar's angel.	
	Judge, O you gods, how dearly Caesar loved him!	
	This was the most unkindest cut of all.	
	For when the noble Caesar saw him stab,	175
	Ingratitude, more strong than traitors' arms,	
	Quite vanquished him. Then burst his mighty heart,	
	And, in his mantle muffling up his face,	
	Even at the base of Pompey's statue	
	(Which all the while ran blood) great Caesar fell.	180
	O, what a fall was there, my countrymen!	
	Then I, and you, and all of us fell down,	
	Whilst bloody treason flourished over us.	
	O, now you weep, and I perceive you feel	
	The dint of pity. These are gracious drops.	185
	Kind souls, what weep you when you but behold	
	Our Caesar's vesture wounded? Look you here,	
	Here is himself, marred as you see with traitors.	
1 PLEBEIAN	O piteous spectacle!	
2 PLEBEIAN	O noble Caesar!	190
3 PLEBEIAN	O woeful day!	
4 PLEBEIAN	O traitors, villains!	
1 PLEBEIAN	O most bloody sight!	
2 PLEBEIAN	We will be revenged!	
ALL	Revenge! About! Seek! Burn! Fire! Kill!	195
	Slay! Let not a traitor live!	
ANTONY	Stay, countrymen.	
1 PLEBEIAN	Peace there, hear the noble Antony.	
2 PLEBEIAN	We'll hear him, we'll follow him, we'll die with him.	
ANTONY	Good friends, sweet friends, let me not stir you up	200
	To such a sudden flood of mutiny.	
	They that have done this deed are honourable.	
	What private griefs they have, alas, I know not,	
	That made them do it. They are wise and honourable,	
	And will no doubt with reasons answer you.	205
	I come not, friends, to steal away your hearts.	
	I am no orator, as Brutus is,	
	But – as you know me all – a plain blunt man	
	That love my friend, and that they know full well	
	That gave me public leave to speak of him.	210
	For I have neither wit, nor words, nor worth,	
	Action, nor utterance, nor the power of speech	
	To stir men's blood. I only speak right on.	
	I tell you that which you yourselves do know,	
	Show you sweet Caesar's wounds, poor, poor, dumb mouths,	215
	And bid them speak for me. But were I Brutus,	
	And Brutus Antony, there were an Antony	
	Would ruffle up your sprits and put a tongue	
	In every wound of Caesar, that should move	
	The stones of Rome to rise and mutiny.	220
ALL	We'll mutiny.	

A Midsummer Night's Dream
Act 4 Scene 1, Lines 43–211
The Wood

Enter PUCK. OBERON *comes forward.*

OBERON Welcome, good Robin. Seest thou this sweet sight?
Her dotage now I do begin to pity;
For, meeting her of late behind the wood 45
Seeking sweet favours for this hateful fool,
I did upbraid her and fall out with her,
For she his hairy temples then had rounded
With coronet of fresh and fragrant flowers;
And that same dew, which sometime on the buds 50
Was wont to swell like round and orient pearls,
Stood now within the pretty flowerets' eyes
Like tears that did their own disgrace bewail.
When I had at my pleasure taunted her,
And she in mild terms begged my patience, 55
I then did ask of her her changeling child,
Which straight she gave me, and her fairy sent
To bear him to my bower in Fairyland.
And now I have the boy, I will undo
This hateful imperfection of her eyes. 60
And, gentle Puck, take this transformèd scalp
From off the head of this Athenian swain,
That, he awaking when the other do,
May all to Athens back again repair,
And think no more of this night's accidents 65
But as the fierce vexation of a dream.
But first I will release the Fairy Queen.

Squeezing a herb on Titania's eyes.

Be as thou wast wont to be;
See as thou wast wont to see.
Dian's bud o'er Cupid's flower 70
Hath such force and blessèd power.
Now, my Titania, wake you, my sweet Queen!

TITANIA *Starting up.*

My Oberon, what visions have I seen!
Methought I was enamoured of an ass.

OBERON There lies your love.

TITANIA How came these things to pass? 75
O, how mine eyes do loathe his visage now!

OBERON Silence awhile: Robin, take off this head.
Titania, music call, and strike more dead
Than common sleep of all these five the sense.

TITANIA Music, ho, music such as charmeth sleep! 80

Soft music plays.

PUCK *[To Bottom, removing the ass's head]*
Now when thou wak'st, with thine own fool's eyes peep.

OBERON Sound, music! Come, my Queen, take hands with me,
And rock the ground whereon these sleepers be.

They dance.

Now thou and I are new in amity,
And will tomorrow midnight solemnly 85
Dance in Duke Theseus' house triumphantly,
And bless it to all fair prosperity.
There shall the pairs of faithful lovers be
Wedded, with Theseus, all in jollity.

PUCK Fairy King, attend, and mark: 90
I do hear the morning lark.

OBERON	Then, my Queen, in silence sad,	
	Trip we after night's shade;	
	We the globe can compass soon,	
	Swifter than the wandering moon.	95
TITANIA	Come, my lord, and in our flight	
	Tell me how it came this night	
	That I sleeping here was found	
	With these mortals on the ground.	

Exeunt OBERON, TITANIA *and* PUCK.

Wind horns. Enter THESEUS *with* HIPPOLYTA, EGEUS, *and all his train.*

THESEUS	Go, one of you, find out the forester;	100
	For now our observation is performed,	
	And since we have the vaward of the day,	
	My love shall hear the music of my hounds.	
	Uncouple in the western valley; let them go:	
	Dispatch, I say, and find the forester.	105

Exit an Attendant.

	We will, fair Queen, up to the mountain's top,	
	And mark the musical confusion	
	Of hounds and echo in conjunction.	
HIPPOLYTA	I was with Hercules and Cadmus once,	
	When in a wood of Crete they bayed the bear	110
	With hounds of Sparta: never did I hear	
	Such gallant chiding; for besides the groves,	
	The skies, the fountains, every region near	
	Seemed all one mutual cry. I never heard	
	So musical a discord, such sweet thunder.	115
THESEUS	My hounds are bred out of the Spartan kind,	
	So flewed, so sanded; and their heads are hung	
	With ears that sweep away the morning dew;	
	Crook-kneed, and dewlapped like Thessalian bulls;	
	Slow in pursuit, but matched in mouth like bells,	120
	Each under each. A cry more tuneable	
	Was never hallooed to nor cheered with horn	
	In Crete, in Sparta, nor in Thessaly.	
	Judge when you hear. But soft, what nymphs are these?	
EGEUS	My lord, this is my daughter here asleep,	125
	And this Lysander; this Demetrius is,	
	This Helena, old Nedar's Helena.	
	I wonder of their being here together.	
THESEUS	No doubt they rose up early to observe	
	The rite of May, and hearing our intent	130
	Came here in grace of our solemnity.	
	But speak, Egeus; is not this the day	
	That Hermia should give answer of her choice?	
EGEUS	It is, my lord.	
THESEUS	Go, bid the huntsmen wake them with their horns.	135

Shout within; wind horns; [the lovers] all start up.

	Good morrow, friends. Saint Valentine is past;	
	Begin these woodbirds but to couple now?	

The lovers kneel.

LYSANDER	Pardon, my lord.	
THESEUS	I pray you all, stand up.	
	I know you two are rival enemies:	
	How comes this gentle concord in the world,	140
	That hatred is so far from jealousy	
	To sleep by hate, and fear no enmity?	
LYSANDER	My lord, I shall reply amazedly,	
	Half sleep, half waking; but as yet, I swear,	
	I cannot truly say how I came here.	145

	But as I think (for truly would I speak)	
	And now I do bethink me, so it is –	
	I came with Hermia hither, Our intent	
	Was to be gone from Athens, where we might	
	Without the peril of the Athenian law –	150
EGEUS	Enough, enough, my lord; you have enough –	
	I beg the law, the law upon his head!	
	They would have stol'n away, they would, Demetrius,	
	Thereby to have defeated you and me,	
	You of your wife, and me of my consent,	155
	Of my consent that she should be your wife.	
DEMETRIUS	My lord, fair Helen told me of their stealth,	
	Of this their purpose hither to his wood;	
	And I in fury hither followed them,	
	Fair Helena in fancy following me.	160
	But, my good lord, I wot not by what power	
	(But by some power it is), my love to Hermia,	
	Melted as the snow, seems to me now	
	As the remembrance of an idle gaud	
	Which in my childhood I did dote upon;	165
	And all the faith, the virtue of my heart,	
	The object and the pleasure of mine eye,	
	Is only Helena. To her, my lord,	
	Was I betrothed ere I saw Hermia;	
	But like a sickness did I loath this food.	170
	But, as in health come to my natural taste,	
	Now I do wish it, love it, long for it,	
	And will for evermore be true to it.	
THESEUS	Fair lovers, you are fortunately met.	
	Of this discourse we more will hear anon.	175
	Egeus, I will overbear your will;	
	For in the temple, by and by, with us	
	These couples shall eternally be knit.	
	And, for the morning now is something worn,	
	Our purposed hunting shall be set aside.	180
	Away with us to Athens. Three and three,	
	We'll hold a feast in great solemnity.	
	Come, Hippolyta.	

Exit THESEUS *with* HIPPOLYTA, EGEUS, *and his train.*

DEMETRIUS	These things seem small and undistinguishable,	
	Like far-off mountains turned into clouds.	185
HERMIA	Methinks I see these things with parted eye,	
	When everything seems double.	
HELENA	So methinks;	
	And I have found Demetrius, like a jewel,	
	Mine own, and not mine own.	
DEMETRIUS	Are you sure	
	That we are awake? It seems to me	190
	That yet we sleep, we dream. Do not you think	
	The Duke was here, and bid us follow him?	
HERMIA	Yea, and my father.	
HELENA	And Hippolyta.	
LYSANDER	And he did bid us follow to the temple.	
DEMETRIUS	Why, then, we are awake. Let's follow him,	195
	And by the way let us recount our dreams.	

Exeunt lovers.

BOTTOM *wakes.*

BOTTOM	When my cue comes, call me, and I will answer. My next is	
	'Most fair Pyramus'. Heigh ho! Peter Quince? Flute the bellows-mender?	
	Snout the tinker? Starveling? God's my life! Stolen hence	
	and left me asleep! I have had a most rare vision. I have had a dream,	200
	past the wit of man to say what dream it was. Man is but	

an ass if he go about to expound this dream. Methought I was – there is no man can tell what. Methought I was – and methought I had – but man is but a patched fool if he will offer to say what methought I had. The eye of man hath not heard, the ear of man hath not seen, man's hand is not able to taste, his tongue to conceive, nor his heart to report what my dream was! I will get Peter Quince to write a ballad of this dream; it shall be called 'Bottom's Dream', because it hath no bottom; and I will sing it in the latter end of a play, before the Duke. Peradventure, to make it the more gracious, I shall sing it at her death.

Exit.